JOHN PILGER has reported from many countries and upheavals for the *Daily Mirror,* the *New Statesman* and Associated Television. He is the only journalist to have been twice named Britain's 'Journalist of the Year': in 1967 for his reporting of the war in Vietnam and in 1979 for his exposé of the suffering of the Cambodian people and their urgent need for world assistance.

ANTHONY BARNETT is an associate of the Trans-National Institute in Amsterdam. He is currently writing a book about the reasons for the rise and fall of the Pol Pot regime. Last year he was a visiting fellow at the Southeast Asia Programme, Cornell University. He is an editor of *New Left Review.*

AFTERMATH
The struggle of Cambodia & Vietnam

ANTHONY BARNETT ■ **JOHN PILGER**

NS REPORT 5

© *Anthony Barnett/John Pilger 1982*

Typeset and designed by
Review Design Services
59 Whitworth St, Manchester 1

Printed by
Manchester Free Press
59 Whitworth St, Manchester 1
061-228 0976

Published by
New Statesman, 10, Great Turnstile, London WC1

ISBN 0 900962 11 9

Trade distribution by
Scottish & Northern Book Distribution Ltd,
18 Granby Row, Manchester 1
&
48A Hamilton Place, Edinburgh EH3 5AX

Southern Distribution
Albion Yard, 17A Balfe Street, London N1

First published in the New Statesman 1978-81

(Date of first publication is given at the end of each article)

Cover photograph—*Eric Piper/Syndication International*

Contents

Introduction

FOR MANY years—for me, it is fifteen years—Anthony Barnett and I have written about and reported from Indochina, from all sides and with subservience to no ideology. Such has been the pattern and the distortion of events during these years, and such has been our own attachment to and admiration for the peoples of the region, that we have found ourselves drawn back, and back, to take up a seemingly unending story of human struggle. It is a story surely unique in our lifetimes and central to any understanding of the wider peril posed to all of us, in the 1980s, by those who 'gave us Vietnam' and whose crimes still await recognition.

So the purpose of publishing the following collection of articles is twofold: first, to enliven memories of the pain endured and the courage displayed during America's pursuit of its 'tragic mistake', which caused the death and maiming and maddening and poisoning and dislocation of millions of human beings and which was no mistake at all; second, to alert the reader to a renewed assault on Vietnam and Cambodia, via American proxies such as Pol Pot's Khmer Rouge, and Peking's 'Pepsi generation', and otherwise malleable international agencies and allied and client governments, using military, economic and propaganda weapons with effect not dissimilar from that of the plagues of helicopter gunships and B52s which flew across our TV screens a decade ago. Remember?

For those who have forgotten, Indochina is where a superpower intervened with almost all its might, short of nuclear weapons (and these *were* contemplated), in order to subdue and subvert and to control nations considered to be of strategic importance to its dominance of world politics. It was beaten; and that had never happened before; and the object of American foreign policy today is to redress this, to gain a 'better result' than that which was declared, ignominiously, on the rooftops of Saigon in April 1975.

The following articles span the last three years, during which the re-writing of recent history in Indochina has been most prolific, from the dissemination of bogus intelligence reports and their acceptance by 'influential' sections of the American media, to the lemming-like acclaim of a celluloid lie, *The Deerhunter*, to the craven attempts to discredit even the *fact* of Pol Pot's crimes against the Khmer people, similar to fascist attempts to deny the Jewish Holocaust. It is this that makes the article, which documents the horrors of the Tuol Sleng concentration camp in Phnom Penh, so important; and I pay tribute to Anthony Barnett's unflagging and scholarly initiative in gathering together documents which clearly show the Khmer Rouge as the Asian Nazis they were, and are. Historians will owe Anthony much for this, for pioneering the direct examination of the regime's own records so that even Ieng Sary could not deny their truth.

Western government propaganda and its foil, functionary journalism, have provided much of the cover for the continuing US 'involvement' in Indochina—now, in effect, a secret war. This secrecy might seem strange in the land that invented 'media wars', with Napalm exploding like giant puffs of blood, on family-time television, between (and at times indistinguishable from) the indigestion remedy commercials. But were not even the massacres conveyed and accepted, if not as 'mistakes', then as 'understandable'? Is not the secret bombing of Cambodia regarded today as the result of Kissinger's and Nixon's venality, not of a system?

For the American public, half the war always remained in shadow; Walter Cronkite never intoned from the moonscape of craters in the north, never saw the forests without birds and the thousands of children in one city, Haiphong, sent permanently deaf from the bombing, nor those in Hanoi's Bach Mai Hospital: the victims of 'Napalm B' which continues to burn beneath the skin through a lifetime. The Agent Orange catastrophe, about which Anthony Barnett writes here and which was perhaps the greatest genetic disaster ever, was seldom reported. My own television films about these subjects were shown throughout the world, but never in the United States.

The secret war began with President Carter who, on assuming office, confronted one central foreign policy problem: how to clean up the image of the United States so that American foreign policy could proceed on its *unchanged* course, which meant 'other Vietnams' in other guises. Carter's selective human rights campaign was part of the solution; and without denying the positive side effects of that policy, especially in the Eastern bloc, the tragic events in Indochina were its greatest 'success'. By adopting the flight of the 'boat people' as a singular human rights crusade, without reference to the American-inspired enforced urbanisation and dislocation complicit in the causes of the exodus, the Carter administration was able to begin to justify past US intervention in Indochina and to clear the way for its repetition, in Asia and elsewhere.

In 1978 Carter described the Pol Pot regime as 'the world's worst violator of human rights'. It was a modest description, appropriately for Carter, for the following year he agreed that the United States should vote for Pol Pot in the United Nations. He encouraged China to arm Pol Pot, the Thais to give him sanctuary and the US-funded aid organisations to provide sustenance and medical care so that his army of executioners could fight again, as the agents of American vengeance and ambitions in Indochina. 'Cambodia thanks US for help at UN', said a headline in the *Washington Post* of August 8, 1980, which reported: 'Premier Khieu Samphan of the deposed Khmer Rouge government of Cambodia has warmly thanked the United States for what he termed its diplomatic support and issued an urgent appeal for aid from Washington and other Western capitals... Mr Samphan and his cabinet have launched a public relations campaign to depict their administration as an innocent and even democratic victim of foreign aggression'.

Now firmly on the side of the 'world's worst violators of human rights' the Carter administration refused all appeals for humanitarian aid to Vietnam, where malnutrition was spreading, and pressed the World Bank to suspend its aid to Vietnam, thus terminating a 60 million dollar loan for an irrigation project which would have increased food production. Britain, the EEC and Japan dutifully cut all aid and loans. Vietnam's isolation was almost complete when, after three and a half years of atrocities across its border by the Chinese-manipulated Khmer Rouge, the Vietnamese army liberated the Khmer people from Pol Pot's charnel house; and I use the word 'liberated' in its purest sense, for while Anthony and I do not suggest in any way that the Vietnamese acted for altruistic reasons—and indeed, for any reasons other than those related to their own survival—every Khmer we met in Cambodia regarded the 'invasion', as it became known in the West, as having saved countless lives, if not the fabric of an entire nation.

That truth hung in the collective gullet of Washington and other Western governments, along with the equally indigestible evidence that Vietnam, virtually alone, was feeding and ministering to the stricken population of Cambodia. Of course, the liberation was to be condemned as an Afghanistan-type invasion—and the waiting angels of the international relief agencies, who waited some seven months before sending substantial aid directly into Cambodia, attempted to cover their own inaction with mumbled accusations of a conspiracy to obstruct, regardless of the enormity of the social and logistical problems existing in the country. Those who apologised for Western governments' and agencies' duplicitous neglect during the early months of death and disorientation remain, on my record, as accessories.

With the ascent of Reagan, official hypocrisy was replaced by a simple, wideeyed monomania about Reds, no matter where, no matter whom. Again, the *Washington Post*: 'The United States has launched a global campaign to punish Vietnam for its invasion of Cambodia by cutting off development assistance from international institutions and curtailing some humanitarian aid'. One of the Reagan administration's first acts was to reject a permit sought by the Mennonite church to send 250 tons of wheat flour to Vietnam, where famine had begun. In April 1981, in Saigon's Pediatric Hospital No. 2, there was less than ten per cent of the milk needed for 400 malnourished patients, most of them children. This hospital's milk supply was cut when the EEC suspended shipments following a shrill campaign led by Margaret Thatcher. The Russians, too, have cut their food aid to Vietnam by 700,000 tons and further reductions are expected. So much for yet another inane label: 'Soviet-backed Vietnam'.

Today, more 'boat people', not surprisingly, are putting to sea: to escape not only the privations of 're-education' but the pervading hunger and poverty for which nothing in their lives has prepared many of them. A large proportion of these people have 'escaped to America', lured by immigrant quotas and by a State Department policy which encourages a continuing exodus as a valuable instrument of 'destabilising' Vietnam, whose economic imprisonment and punishment is to be, it appears, at the pleasure of whomever occupies the White House.

'The United States under President Reagan will continue to bring the maximum pressure to bear on Vietnam. Unless the Vietnamese feel pain, they'll have no incentive to leave Kampuchea'—*John Holdridge, Assistant Secretary of State for East Asia.*

'I don't really know the Vietnamese. I am indifferent towards them. What I know, and every Khmer knows, is that *only* they stand between us and the return of the Pol Pot nightmare'—*Pak Samrin, a Phnom Penh teacher whose family of six died violently under Pol Pot.*

'Our friends in the world are the United Nations... Thailand and Singapore, and the United States. Oh, yes the United States!'—*Nam Phann, Khmer Rouge base commander at Phnom Chat on the Thai border, known to Western aid officials as 'Pol Pot's Himmler' and 'The Butcher'.*

'There are some things more important than peace'—*General Alexander Haig, US Secretary of State.*

John Pilger
London, October 1981

Part I
Vietnam

Back to Vietnam
John Pilger

My last glimpse of the Vietnam I knew so well, for so long, was from the deck of an American aircraft carrier in the South China Sea. It was a blazing tropical dusk of which the now-we-say farewell travelogues used to be made; and the scene on the USS *Blue Ridge* which had received those of us who had chosen to exit gracelessly by helicopter in the last hours of the last day, said much about the longest war game of the twentieth century. Sailors, marines and pilots lounged; reporters moped, like homeward bound conventioneers; the poodle belonging to and much beloved by the last American ambassador to Vietnam, Graham Martin, took its evening walk among the F-5 fighters and the Jolly Green Giant gunships, accompanied by the ambassador's Vietnamese manservant, who also hovered with a plastic trowel; the last CIA station chief in Saigon, Thomas Polgar, who had managed to struggle on board with an illicit cache of Scotch, stared Buddha-like at the horizon. (It was Polgar who, in defiance of Graham Martin, had ordered the giant tamarind tree in the embassy grounds to be chopped down so that the Jolly Green Giants could land and complete the evacuation. Martin, an ailing recluse with symptoms of martyrdom, had proclaimed, 'Once that great tree falls and they see that we are running for our lives, all American prestige will fall with it.') And round and round the vast deck jogged a platoon of playful marines, spurting at each exhortation from their sergeant for 'a big dirty dozen, you guys!' The marines jogged past the ship's rock band, which was tuning up for that evening's end-of-term celebrations, past the portable barbecue sets on to which chefs were hoisting slabs of prime cut steak; crates of Coke and Diet Cola had already arrived—but, alas, no booze: American naval ships are 'dry' and this fact was bemoaned over the PA by the Admiral himself, a jovial, obese man in a cap who looked and spoke like the late Andy Devine. 'Well folks', said he, 'that just about wraps up Vietnam. So let's all have a party and get outta here, so we can mosey on back to Subic Bay and get ourselves a genuine Budweiser beer!'

The admiral's voice, the joggers' heavings, the band's inanities and the clatter of the feast preparations all but drowned a persistent knocking at our stern, as though someone was trying to bring us all to order. 'Damned if it ain't *them*!' said a marine major, peering over the side, 'damned if it ain't the gooks.' About fifty Vietnamese huddled below us in a listing, ruined landing craft; they were mostly

CHINA

Dien Bien Phu

Hanoi

North
Vietnam

LAOS

Vinh

DMZ
Quang Tri
Hue
Danang

THAILAND

CAMBODIA

Saigon

South
Vietnam

0   50   100
    miles

families and at least a third of them were children. They were part of a flotilla of small boats that had come after us, having been told for a generation to fear for their lives under the communists. For most of that day, in the great heat, an old man had swung a boathook laced up with pots and pans against the carrier's side, while another attempted to heave a length of rope up on to the deck; it barely reached aboard, anyway there was no one to catch it; the few times it appeared the joggers jogged over it. As the first steaks were devoured and the dreadful band struck up, the *Blue Ridge* shuddered and moved forward, leaving the exhausted faces still pleading to be taken on board. A box of Diet Cola was thrown down to them, but it missed and sank. They had been given, we were assured, five days' supply of fresh water and a map; that their wretched craft was already sinking and they would go nowhere, except down, was acknowledged; but still we steamed away. A few hours earlier a few of us had watched as the bodies of two infants were lowered into the sea; and in one last, disconsolate gesture, which is embedded in my memory, a woman stood up and held out her baby as if to say, 'At least take him!'; then she slipped and they both fell into the sea. I and other reporters wrote about that small finale, but it was published in only a few American papers. By the time we reached the Philippines and telex machines and got ourselves a genuine Budweiser beer, Vietnam was indeed 'just about wrapped up'. The world's first media war had simply run out of ratings, and little has been heard from there in the intervening three and a half years. This summer I went back, and some impressions follow. The above preface is, I believe, a necessary reminder of how the game was played.

Close by the runway at Hanoi airport, the words *'Dai Thang'* are emblazoned on a hoarding raised on the rim of a bomb crater so large it has been improved with steps and in a field where twisted, moss-overgrown metal, the remains of a pulverised train, protrudes almost as sculpture. *Dai Thang* means 'Great Victory' and some people here still proffer a greeting that entered the language on April 30, 1975—'Welcome to the Great Victory', although this is much less popular now as the realities of the war's aftermath chasten the memory of that heady day when the people of Hanoi filled the streets, at first in silence, incredulous at the brief announcement that their thirty-year war was over. Indeed, the Homeric hoardings are the only sign that this is 'the nation that beat the giant' and arriving here is almost like stumbling on the appendage to some great and unrecorded disaster. For all the media saturation of the war in the south only half the war and half the story were reported; I, for one, never imagined what was happening here.

Much of North Vietnam is a moonscape from which visible signs of life—houses, factories, schools, hospitals, pagodas, churches—have been obliterated. In some forests there are no longer birds and animals; and there are lorry drivers who will not respond to the hooting of a horn because they are deaf from the incessant sound of bombs; according to the Vice Minister of Health, more than 30,000 children in Hanoi and Haiphong suffered permanent deafness during the twelve nights of bombings at Christmas 1972. In Hanoi's Bach Mai Hospital, doctors have discovered that Napalm 'B', an amalgam of benzine, polystyrene and gasoline, which the Dow Chemical Company created especially for Vietnam, continues to smoulder under the skin's tissues through the lifetime of its victims. Perhaps more evidence that this was a war of rampant technology against people is hardly needed; but the evidence is here, in the north, in its unexpurgated form, along with the truth that the war was 'won', if that word applies at all, not by Oriental Prussians under the spell of an ideology (North Vietnam was never like

China; the Vietnamese by nature are sceptics and often cranky individualists) but by a peasant people who developed their ingenuity and patience to the extreme human limits and were united in their sense of community and history. It is this extraordinary presence of history, during which they have repelled the Chinese, the Mongols, the Siamese, the Japanese, the French and the Americans, that now dominates the ironic and seemingly baffling shuffles in present Vietnamese foreign policy—but more about that later. One of the most moving stories I was told about them came from a Frenchman who was in Hanoi during the 1972 bombing. 'I took shelter in the museum', he said, 'and there, working by candlelight with the B52s overhead, were young men and women earnestly trying to copy as many bronzes and sculptures as they could. They told me, "Even if the originals are destroyed, *something* will remain and our roots will be protected".' In Hanoi Zoo, the wreckage of twenty-three B52s shot down during Christmas 1972 is kept in a cage under a conventional zoological sign showing a map of the United States and the words 'Great Ferocious Beast'. Children peering through the bars at it chorus 'Beefeetytoo!' and make a mock growling noise. Nothing, not even the power of irony, is wasted here.

But all this appears unreal because Hanoi today is no more than a gentle, monkish Asian backwater of controlled poverty. There are no beggars, but if you throw away the stick of your ice lolly it is likely that a hovering person will retrieve it and wash it and press it into some other service: *that* is how they survived. Thirty years of war have exterminated private cars and taxis; this is a city silent with the bicycle, one of which is mounted in a hallowed corner of the museum; on it, a man and 300 kilos of supplies peddled distances of up to 500 miles in order to win that other 'great victory', at Dien Bien Phu. Most of Hanoi's people still live in narrow streets laid out as in the Middle Ages on a craft basis: streets of workers in ivory, brass and leather, streets of tinsmiths, streets of coffin-makers. These streets, not the spacious, French-built centre, were the B52s' main target and 'carpets' of bombs were laid down them with sustained accuracy. In Kham Thiem Street, at ten o'clock on Boxing Night 1972, a bomb hit every third house; and every day since an old nicotine-stained figure has kept a vigil at one of these gaps, in a state of enduring wonder at his own survival. His name is Hoang Van Dung and he alone lived where 283 died. 'It was a block of flats', he said, 'we were mostly the old, women and children. There was no time to reach the shelters, and we sang as the bombs came down.'

Route One, going south to Saigon and branching west to the Ho Chi Minh Trail (to which foreign tour parties are planned), is the 'Street of No Joy': a nickname shared, with equal good reason, by the people who depended on its convoys and the American pilots who blitzed it. There were no SAM missiles here, just militia of local people who would put up a curtain of small arms fire as the F105s and the Phantoms came in at 200 feet; and when the planes had gone, small groups of mostly women and children would swim the pontoons into place to allow the trucks through, then dismantle them before dawn and hide them in the paddies. Today, most villages have their own museum of US Air Force scrap: a pilot's helmet, a boot, a Batman comic. At Dong Loc, which was bombed back to the Stone Age and beyond, leaving craters that have merged into a swamp, are the graves of the entire anti-aircraft militia, all young women ... Vo Thi Than, aged 22, Duong Thi Tan, aged 19. A place called Ham Long ought to be as famous as Dresden, because it was bombed more than Dresden: every day for four years, from five in the morning till two in the afternoon. It is overlooked by a mangy hill on which, inexplicably, anti-aircraft gunners are still dug in. 'Maybe', said my guide, 'they don't believe it is *really* over'.

Through all this, life proceeded in astonishing ways. What now appear as archaeological digs were underground hospitals: wards, operating theatres, baby delivery rooms. Every village in North Vietnam had its own *crèche,* and as the planes swept in from the sea the infants were lowered on a cord and pulley device four at a time, each in separate padded baskets, into deep shelters just below their cribs; and in every classroom, beside every desk, was a trap door so that within seconds a class of fifty children would literally disappear. In this way, casualties outside the towns were kept low. However, in Vinh, a large mining community, the layer upon layer of bombing penetrated underground and today not even the foundations of buildings remain. Vinh is flanked by a saddle of hills and evokes the haunting photograph of Hiroshima taken on the first anniversary of the atomic bombing. People here, living under straw, are today on the edge of famine; a Cuban agronomist I met told me that, because of two crop failures and the sudden union of two alien economies that had thrown distribution into chaos, people living in devastated areas, such as Vinh, were being rationed to just six pounds of rice per *month*. 'That is considerably less than Bangladesh', he reminded me. On the day I was in Vinh, a long military convoy rumbled through the streets of straw. The soldiers in the lorries were conscripted teenagers and I learned later that they were going to the war on the border with Cambodia; they represent Vietnam's third consecutive generation at war. And as I proceeded south, I learned that American-made F-5 and A-37 planes were flying regular missions over Cambodia, mostly from Bien Hoa base, and dropping 250-pound bombs and anti-personnel 'cluster' bombs which discharge thousands of small needles and, like Napalm, were developed by the Americans especially for their war in Vietnam. At the same time, Vietnamese ground commanders are using American-made helicopters to collect the wounded and they are placing military significance on a 'body count' of enemy dead. None of this is a re-enactment for Hollywood cameras; not only are the Vietnamese using American equipment, they have also adopted American tactics and jargon: 'air-strikes', 'gunships', 'body count', etc. The conflict with Cambodia, or Democratic Kampuchea as it is now known, has much to do with who controls the disputed ricelands of the 'Parrots Beak' and with regional animosities that have simmered for thousands of years. With their air strikes and gunships and body counts, the Vietnamese are trying to overthrow the present regime in Phnom Penh and to replace it with one less inclined towards China and more malleable to Vietnam's wishes. Names and places are different, and roles are reversed; but have we not read all this before?

The old South Vietnam begins at Quang Tri, on the seventeenth parallel, where Vietnam was divided into two 'national regrouping areas' by the 1954 Geneva Conference on Incochina. The hills here, with scabrous crowns that once were fire bases, look like miniature extinct volcanoes; and, as with so many places in the south I knew well during the war, the realisation that I had been here before was slow in coming. Apart from one shell-pocked shrine, there is nothing to indicate that for five years thousands of US Marines were dug into these hills, utterly isolated in warrens of mud and dust, often lying painfully on their sides and often in their own shit and blood, under orders not to advance an inch forward but to 'sustain' the artillery, mortar fire and rockets that pummelled them day and night. This was the Demilitarised Zone, the DMZ; when I came here in 1967 the rotors of the helicopter that brought me were blown away, causing me to spend four days

Eric Piper/Syndication International

Ex-Vietcong Minh No. 4 shows off part of the 200 mile network of tunnels at Cu Chi, 50 miles from Saigon, which was used as a central staging point by the Vietcong during the war.

instead of the few hours I had planned. They were all volunteers, of whom the majority were poor whites weaned on John Wayne, and blacks in retreat from the ghetto. Their frustration was intolerable; they were here not as soldiers but as targets, to be hit and maimed and killed. On the helicopter that lifted me out were three dead and two dying. Surely men have not often demonstrated such raw bravery in the cause of nothing. And today there is not a single grave here: not a helmet or a boot.

The 'graves' begin a few miles beyond these hills. Not American graves; there are none in Vietnam. Nor even graves with human remains. At the end of the war, the men in Hanoi gave priority to a cosmetics operation that perhaps has no parallel anywhere, in its intent and scope. Throughout South Vietnam—where, in the last years of the war, whole armoured divisions of the North Vietnamese Army usurped the role of the southern National Liberation Front (the Vietcong) and engaged in set-piece battles—there are now hundreds of military cemeteries that did not exist three and a half years ago. These cemeteries are phoney. They were prefabricated in the north and transported to those battlefields on which the North Vietnamese fought and lost many. Each new headstone has the name of the soldier purported to be resting beneath it; he is not. The North Vietnamese Army was meticulous about gathering up its dead, and had units trained especially for the job, so that the *Bo Dai* ('soldiers of liberation') could be buried with honours in the north. The cemeteries in the south are both symbols of grief and defiance; one of them has been raised on a bulldozed American base, whose ashes—tyres, shell casings, a Coke machine, a volleyball net—have been swept ignominiously into one neat tip.

At Hue, the old imperial capital for which the North Vietnamese and the Americans mauled each other and the civilian population for thirty-six days and nights during *Tet* in 1968, my guide, a melancholic man called Do Tuan That, refused to walk with me through the citadel. He said he would cross the moat but not enter the garden. As a young lieutenant in the NVA, he had been here through the most intense holocaust of the war and he clearly regarded his survival as a miracle; he is today terribly scarred and infested with shrapnel, and it was not difficult to understand his reluctance. The citadel is today as though a swarm of especially virulent locusts descended on it and savaged every tree; even the ancient walls appear to have been 'eaten'. One landscaped terrace, where the first line of NVA troops was dug in, has resisted all attempts to implant it, and is now considered to be poisoned for the foreseeable future.

Directly opposite, across the Perfume River, is a hotel built in 1962 for the first American advisers to the Diem regime. Beneath a plastic chandelier there is a long padded bar, now frequented by a few *cadres* but mostly by Russians, East Germans and Cubans who, with splendid and unwitting irony, use virtually the same vocabulary of derision to describe their hosts as the Americans used before them. One particular Russian, a senior technocrat, even looked like one of his American predecessors: crew cut, tailored safari suit, patent shoes, fine Samsonite attache case. He did not use the word 'gooks' but the message of his sentiments was clear. 'These people', he said, 'infuriate me; they are lazy, dirty, incompetent, ungrateful and they will not listen when you tell them how to manage themselves. And the controls! They have people spying on us everywhere, telling us how to do this, do that. I am despairing of them. Look at my position; I am here to help them, but they are full of suspicion; they restrict my movements. I am fed up with them... aaah!' A Cuban seated beside him approved of this diatribe. 'They're impossible', he said, 'they won't be told *anything*.'

I bumped into this pair in Danang and Saigon and each time their griping rose to a new crescendo. I also met several East Germans who, although less vocal in their complaining, confirmed the restrictions placed on them as advisers. All this was most interesting, because it strongly suggested that the basic lesson of Vietnam's long struggle is still to be learnt by her allies as it was learnt painfully by her adversaries: that the Vietnamese passion for independence, coupled with a fear of subjugation by war or by aid-with-strings, transcends so-called fraternalism.

Today, the main thrust of Vietnamese foreign policy is to make friends with the United States and with member countries of the Western-leaning ASEAN alliance. The secretary of the Vietnamese Communist Party, Xuan Thuy, startled Washington by offering unconditional commercial and diplomatic ties with America and said that Vietnam no longer would insist on American reconstruction aid and reparations. This was repeated to a visiting group of American Congressmen in increasingly desperate tones. The Vietnamese not only want American technology and capital investment (while I was in Hanoi, a fraternal delegation from East Germany was moved out of the best hotel to make room for a fraternal delegation from the Chase Manhattan Bank) but, above all, they want to extricate Vietnam from the cold war between Moscow and Peking. The Vietnamese say that there are some 10,000 Chinese bolstering the Cambodian war effort and, as that war intensifies, the belief is growing in Hanoi that the Chinese will mount a limited invasion from either of its two military regions that border Vietnam and where there are as many divisions as there are in the entire Vietnamese army. This might be averted, runs their reasoning, if Vietnamese diplomats are ensconced in Washington and can persuade the Americans to exercise their now considerable influence on the Chinese.

Readers might wish to pause here to consider the kaleidoscope of ironies in all this. Why did John Foster Dulles, in sabotaging the Geneva Conference in 1954, prevent the establishment of a United Vietnam all those wasted years ago? To contain Chinese communism, of course! For those like myself, who do not play chess, keeping up with the game of nations in the Seventies has its difficulties; but what all this comes down to, it seems clear, is that if America had left Indochina alone, Vietnam would have evolved quickly into what it is now attempting to become: an Asian Yugoslavia, fiercely independent and on reasonable, self-interested terms with its region and with most of the world. That the American war merely delayed this process, and in the meantime caused the death and maiming of several million people and the technological vandalism of a nation and its land, not to mention the current enslavement of the Khmer people, is for sure the saddest truth of my time.

Danang, where the Marines stormed ashore Hollywood-style in 1965 and which became a pen of dislocated humanity fleeing from General Westmoreland's 'free fire zones', as well as the greatest whorehouse in Asia, displays its bitterness more than Saigon. 'Fuck you!' and 'You number ten, pig!' wafted at me over lattice walls. From here, Combined Action Company units—better known as WHAM boys—went west into the highlands and set up strategic camps and, with their WHAM handbooks to guide them (P82: 'Never pat a Vietnamese on the head'), distributed everything from chocolate bars to electric flush lavatories. WHAM stood for winning hearts and minds and its missionaries were usually combat-weary marines, survivors of the DMZ; inevitably, much of their largesse found its way to the Vietcong. WHAM country is now a New Economic Zone, where soldiers, politicians, civil servants and hucksters of the old regime are employed in the paddies and in clearing land. Many are called 'volunteers'; in practice, this means that 'non-producers', such as bankrupt small businessmen who have no choice but to plead poverty to the authorities, are directed to lorries that leave for the countryside before sunrise every morning. In one new 'co-operative'—only a few miles from where, eleven years before, I spent a week with Sergeant Melvin Murrell's WHAM unit and watched incredulous peasants receive packets of Uncle Ben's miracle processed rice, comics and 5,000 toothbrushes—there are several hundred former Saigon soldiers pressed into a harsh rural existence, for which nothing in their life has prepared them.

And consider this mighty irony: the Vietnamese Government has applied to the World Bank for a loan. The World Bank is headed by Robert MacNamara, the former hawkish Defence Secretary under Lyndon Johnson, from whom came the inspiration for an electrified fence around South Vietnam that would 'sanitise the nation against the disease of communism.' The World Bank is almost certain to help Vietnam, at least partly because MacNamara is reportedly impressed with the concept of the New Economic Zones as 'essential to the economic recovery of a proud nation'.

These zones and the 're-education' programme are entwined. It is difficult to know with certainty who is sent off to the countryside to be re-educated, how long they must spend there and if they return. Few high-ranking military officers have returned. One young woman I met told me that her father, an army surgeon, had been taken away a few days after the fall of Saigon and the family had received no news of him; even their repeated requests for confirmation that he is alive have

Eric Piper/Syndication International

Vietnam: American tanks left behind after the war.

been refused. However, her brother-in-law, an architect, returned after two years of re-education, leaner but otherwise well, and was immediately allowed to practise his profession. He had played the re-education game skilfully by not complaining and by feigning 'confessions' of past political allegiances, and after a while the family was permitted to write a letter to him every two months. They were given a number and a postcode and in their letters they always included effusive words of praise for Uncle Ho's wisdoms—which they hoped would speed his release.

He described a rigorous ten-hour day clearing land near the border with Cambodia. His food was frugal: a mush of rice and animal fodder; and he slept in barracks he had helped to build. There was little brutality, but suicides among the oldest were not uncommon, and there was much suffering from untreated dysentry and malaria. The rationale behind the zones is only partly political and punitive. The government has said that some ten million people are to be moved over the next twenty years from the cities to the underpopulated mountainous areas in the north and west, facing the two current enemies: Cambodia and China.

Another reason is the critical food situation. The beginnings of famine I saw in Vinh, in the north, are no aberration. Vietnam's area of cultivation has remained exactly what it was under King Hung 4000 years ago; but in the meantime the population has leapt to 50 million, to which a million and a half mouths are added each year. During the war years, North Vietnam subsisted like a Trappist practising self-denial while South Vietnam, the former rice bowl, sustained an exodus to the cities and was fed intravenously by the Americans, who pulled out the tubes when they flew away. Food, or the lack of it, is obsessively discussed; at one neighbourhood re-education session there were muffled complaints about the bureaucracy's poor record of distribution. 'You should not complain,' said a humourless *cadre,* 'it's better than before when the Americans ate the flesh of your babies!' At this, an old woman leapt to her feet and shouted, 'Rubbish! We all know the Americans only eat out of cans!' The audience burst into laughter and cheering, relishing the moment of rebellion. Re-educating millions of like-minded heretics will not be easy.

Throughout South Vietnam, northerners are firmly in control at all but the lowest level of administration: the neighbourhood committee, or *To,* whose chief apparatchik is seldom a veteran of NLF. Whenever I put the question, 'What has happened to the Vietcong?' the response invariably would be: 'They are in positions of responsibility,' or, less obliquely, 'A great many died in the liberation struggle'. The latter, of course, is true; by the end of the direct American involvement, the Americans, with their massive firepower, had indeed achieved their aim of a high 'kill ratio', especially in the Mekong Delta. In Saigon, I attended an 'evening of culture' in the former National Assembly, which the French built as an opera house; the tableaux of song and dance had the repetitive theme of liberation fighters entering Saigon to an ecstatic welcome by the people—which, of course, did not happen. In the intermission, a young man hovering close to me whispered, 'Do you like our revolutionary theatre?' 'Yes,' I responded, dutifully. 'Well, mister, I hope you enjoy it, these actors are all you'll see of the VC!'

The VC I met are now tourist guides. One of them, a Mr Dung, conducted me around the former presidential palace where Thieu cowered in his bunker until he wisely sought the political calm of Wimbledon, where he lives today. Mr Dung invited me to sit in Thieu's grandiose throne and was amused when I told him that the last time I was in the palace was to report a ceremony in which Spiro Agnew, then Vice-President of the United States, presented Thieu with a gift-wrapped filing cabinet '… as a token of the esteem of the American people'. The throne, inlaid with gold and ivory, is behind a large desk and raised on a platform so that, in the immortal words of Graham Martin, the last American pro-consul, 'whenever the little bastard received us we didn't have to pat him on the head'.

I was taken to see a place I had heard many rumours about during the war, including one that it did not exist: the Vietcong's 'central staging point' at Cu Chi, fifty miles from Saigon. It existed all right: it is a remarkable network of tunnels, 200 miles of them, through which whole regiments slid like snakes during daytime, emerging at night to re-supply and to ambush. The Americans were never able to find or destroy the main tunnels, even though the tunnels were situated less than a Sunday drive from the great jukebox that was the US command complex in Saigon, where a procession of air-conditioned generals saw the fabled light at the end of their own metaphoric tunnels. 'Operation Hades' was conceived in the late Sixties to root out the subterranean enemy, and tracts of forest were defoliated and crops were poisoned in the process. After an American Academy of Sciences team came to Vietnam and discovered that the aerial spraying of herbicides, long banned in the United States, was also producing deformed babies, the name was changed to the more friendly and acceptable 'Operation Ranch Hand'.

The main entrance to the tunnels is a large trapdoor ringed by petrified trees, beyond which shimmers an horizon laid completely to waste 'for maybe half a century or more', according to one Academy member's report to Congress. (The Vietnamese estimate that 44 per cent of the country's forests have been similarly destroyed.) When five of us arrived at Cu Chi, a bizarre and touching little scene awaited us; against this nuclear horizon, within sight of a bomb crater, a wrecked American tank, a shallow grave and a crippled child drawing water with a Napalm canister, a lunch table was being laid. The tablecloth was white linen, silver cutlery was wrapped in pink napkins, beer stood in ice buckets and cold towels were dispensed with deference by a waiter who also saw off the flies and mosquitoes.

A nugget of a man with two red stars on his collar greeted us. 'My name is Minh Number Four!' he said 'I am the leader here. We want you to enjoy your visit. We are proud of Cu Chi.' Minh Number Four—that's his military codename—came down from the north in 1961 and he and his men lived and fought literally in darkness for a decade; indeed, his eyes are still those of a hypogeal creature recently released into the light. Today, the tunnels are inhabited by insect mutations, created by the herbicides; crouched in a shaft less than three feet high, Minh said, 'During daylight the Americans would be directly above. To shoot them we often had to trip them up first, to get the right aim. We killed them one by one.' How did he regard the Americans now? 'I feel sorry for them,' he replied. 'They underestimated our abilities very badly; they thought we were children who could be brushed aside in a year or two.'

Saigon remains in shock. The greatest consumer society in the world that produced nothing (except an estimated 1800 dollar millionaires) is like an old whore with a hangover; and not all the girls with the steel skin and the ladled mascara and the tight white pants are off being re-educated; some of them have been kept on for the services of the *Bo Dai,* though at much reduced rates. A Saigon without beggars and junkies and 'dust of life' urchins and double amputee veterans coming at you like crabs with a sawn off Coke can, is now a pleasant city which manages to mask its tensions and frustrations.

A villa that was the CIA's Saigon headquarters has been converted to the world's first Disneyland of carnage; and at the end of your tour you are given tea to relieve the nausea brought on by the unrelenting horror of the displays. Every devilish thing that was dropped on them is here including a bomb that sucked the oxygen from the air, killed people and left buildings intact: a miniature neutron bomb no less. There is a weed developed by American scientists to prevent anything else from growing. There is a CIA relief map of Saigon's brothels that lights up. There is a reconstruction of the 'tiger cages' of Con Son Island and a beautiful, crippled young woman called Tao, who will tell you how cold water was thrown into her cage during winter and quick-lime in summer. 'You don't imagine', she said, 'when I hear the war is over, my mind flies.' When Tran Van Tuyen heard the war was over, did his mind fly, too? He was chairman of the National Assembly and one of the most tenacious democrats I ever knew. A radical lawyer of the 'third force', he poured his limitless compassion into helping Thieu's political prisoners until, he, too, was imprisoned in the tiger cages and was tortured, which once included burial to his neck in sewage. He is now said to be officially classified as 'obstinate' and has been despatched to some miserable place for re-education.

One wall of photographs in this 'war crimes museum' is devoted to 'Operation Babylift', that squalid episode shortly before the end of the war when hundreds of waifs, many of them not orphans, were bundled out of Saigon in the cause of newspaper circulation, dubious charitable motives and the fraudulent image of Richard Nixon's successor. Those who will recall the assault on their emotions particularly when 150 babies died in the crash of an American 'mercy plane', will be pleased to learn that the orphans and handicapped children left behind are being well cared for—and with a sensitivity that covers equally the small nation fathered by Americans. These children are given a compassionate unembellished story of their origins: they are told that their fathers were foreign soldiers who had to go home; there is no mention of war crimes or 'imperialist aggressors'; and if their mother can be found and she has an address in America, as sometimes happens, they are encouraged to write to their fathers. They are even taught some 'American culture', and Donald Duck shares the wall above their beds with Uncle Ho. The generosity and total absence of rancour embodied in the official approach to bringing up these children of the former enemy is the other side to a regime that indulges its Stalinism in the intellectual barbarities of 're-education'. At the Young Flower orphanage in Saigon I asked the name of a black curly-headed jumping ball with big Chicago eyes. 'My name is Tran,' he said. 'I am nine.' I asked him, 'What are the words of the song you have just sung?' He looked gravely at the floor, as kids do, and his words left the interpreter shaking her head. She repeated slowly: 'The war is gone... planes come no more... do not weep for those just born... the human being is evergreen.'

(15 September 1978)

The Chinese invasion
Anthony Barnett

China invaded Vietnam on Saturday 18 February 1979. This article was written on
Sunday 19 February and published on 23 February, when the war was underway.

When Zbigniew Brzezinski visited Peking in May 1978 and set in train the
'normalisation' of Sino-American relations (which for the Chinese means a virtual
alliance with the United States), Deng Xiaoping told him that he saw Vietnam as
'the Asian Cuba'. As an analogy drawn by the leader of a socialist country, it ought
to have been quite a compliment. But what happened to Cuba when its revolution
displeased its immense northern neighbour? It was attacked at the Bay of Pigs,
embargoed and denounced for its dependence on the USSR. Thus, Deng's
description is little more than a vanity. By denouncing Vietnam as an 'Asian Cuba'
he implied that China was the 'Asian United States'.

There is little doubt that China regards Southeast Asia as its own sphere of
influence. Were it in a position to do so, it would declare a 'Monroe Doctrine' for
the lands to its south. Vietnam's position astride the land bridge to Southeast Asia
proper has precipitated what must be the most fantastic and may be the most
irreconcilable territorial dispute on the globe today. The map overleaf shows
China's claims on the sea area to its south, regarded as its 'territory' because of
occasional reefs breaking through the waters right down to Indonesia. At present
both China and Vietnam lay claim to the two major groups of islands, the Paracels
and the Spratlys. Peking occupies the first and Vietnam most of the second. But
the dispute is not simply over islands. China's claims to the seabed extend over a
vast area south of the Spratlys, where oil deposits hold out the prospect of
economic independence for Vietnam.

Relations between the two countries began to deteriorate as long ago as 1954, at
the Geneva Conference. It was there that Vietnam was divided and Chou En-lai,
as we have since learnt from the *Pentagon Papers*, played a decisive role with the
carving knife.

Chou (and Mao) sought three main objectives at Geneva. First, they wanted to
neutralise Indochina and rid it of the threat of American troops. Second, they
hoped this would enable them to break the military encirclement of China by

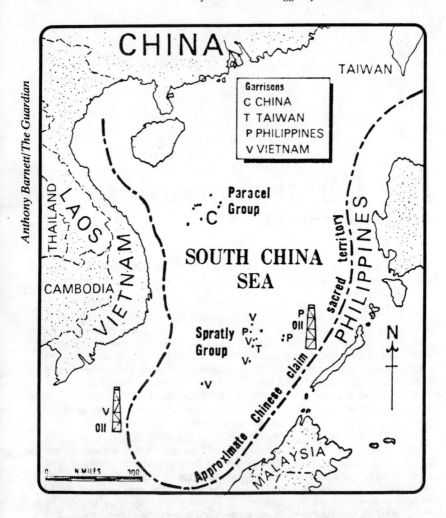

means of an international treaty, which in turn would also allow them to break out of their diplomatic isolation and forced dependence on the Russians. Finally, if they could achieve this by acting as the guarantor of neutral states such as Sihanouk's Cambodia, while dividing Vietnam, their suzerainity would be complete. Chou secretly informed the French that he recognised the reality of the South Vietnamese government they were attempting to construct. His plans misfired—with the ironic result that his country's diplomatic isolation was only ended when the war that followed between Vietnam and the United States looked like being won by a Vietnamese party no longer beholden to Peking.

Nixon's visit to Peking in 1972 can be taken as *the* major breaking point. He sought then to return to the Geneva agreement as the Chinese had conceived it—and found a willing response. Almost certainly, both Nixon and Mao wanted the Paris Peace Accords to last, and therefore Vietnam to remain divided. The Vietnamese victory in 1975 was thus a defeat for Chinese foreign policy, as well as for Nixon's. And as the final liberation of South Vietnam took place, Mao Tse Tung sourly informed his entourage: 'The Soviet Union has wild ambitions. It wants to lay hands on the whole of Europe, Asia and Africa'.

A year earlier, Mao had ordered that the Paracel Island group be seized from a small garrison of Thieu's South Vietnamese troops. It was a highly significant move: for the first time, the Chinese escalated their disagreements with Hanoi to the level of force. At the same time, the two countries shared a common position on Cambodia, albeit for different reasons—so there was no 'provocation' on Vietnam's part, no 'regional hegemonism', no 'expansionism' which needed to be 'punished' (these being the expressions used by China in the current conflict). The islands guard the sea route to Hanoi: it was at once a brutal humiliation and an ominous warning. If China was willing to exploit Vietnam's weakness, when it was still divided and in struggle against the Thieu regime, then China was capable of anything.

After the liberation of Saigon, Le Duan, the General Secretary of the Vietnamese Communist party visited Peking before going on to Moscow. Disagreement was so complete that no return banquet was held nor any communiqué issued. Obviously, the role of the Soviet Union was one matter that divided Le Duan and Mao: it must have seemed ludicrous to the Vietnamese that the USSR should be regarded as the main enemy, when it had been their major source of support. But there was another crucial issue at stake. As Hanoi's representative left China, Peking republished in the most emphatic terms its claims on the South China Sea.

The following year, just a few months after Mao died, his successors dealt a heavy blow to Vietnam's Communist pride by boycotting the Fourth Party Congress in Hanoi. This was the Congress of victory, of unification and, the Vietnamese hoped above all, of peace. Hindsight gives two other aspects of that Congress a special significance. First, the Cambodians also boycotted it, in what was evidently a co-ordinated action with Peking's. Second, the Soviet Union put overt pressure on the Vietnamese to join COMECON, and was rebuffed. Hanoi was still determined to pursue its policy of maximising independence through conducting an even-handed approach to all socialist countries and calling for them to work together. For Peking, this was simply anathema. Not only did it mean a flat rejection of its cherished anti-Sovietism, but it also challenged Peking's own vanity as a world influence, for Vietnam's was a policy far more attractive to developing nations.

Just over two years later, China caused Vietnam to abandon its policy of multiple-relations. As Vietnam's Foreign Minister put it when he visited Tokyo in December 1978, 'we are sacrificing our independent policy somewhat', because of the 'about face' of the country's northern neighbour. Having forced Vietnam into a binding treaty with Moscow, China then invaded it.

Cambodia was, of course, the immediate *casus belli*. Here another analogy has been drawn, even less apposite than the Cuban one: the Vietnamese action in Cambodia has been compared to the Soviet invasion of Czechoslovakia. Almost all observers agree that there had been low level friction between Vietnam and Cambodia after their mutual revolutions in 1975, but that in March and April of 1977 the fighting escalated, with serious attacks by the Khmer Rouge on Vietnamese border villages, killing some hundreds of their inhabitants. Did the Czechs ever attack the Soviet Union?

In February 1978, after its own counter-assault, Hanoi issued a three-point peace proposal. It suggested that all troops be withdrawn five miles from the frontier; that Vietnam and Cambodia discuss and resolve their differences (including a disagreement over the border); and that there be international inspection of the cease-fire. If one can imagine Brezhnev making such an offer to the Czechs, one can be sure Dubcek would have accepted. Pol Pot declined to do so.

The conflict between Vietnam and Cambodia was never a 'proxy war' between the USSR and China as Brzezinski has claimed. On the contrary, the determining conflict was between Vietnam and China, with all other conflicts organised around that focal point. Neither Peking nor Hanoi however wanted open antagonism: both feared it would have incalculable consequences (as indeed they are now beginning to discover). It was against their better judgement that developments in Cambodia, which were of secondary importance to each of them, detonated a major confrontation between the two countries.

If we are to understand how this extraordinary set of conflicts came about, it is necessary to put them into an order of causality. When Pol Pot consolidated his position in Democratic Kampuchea by placing Sihanouk under 'Palace arrest' at the beginning of April 1976, his action followed upon the death of Chou En-lai, who had been Sihanouk's patron, and coincided with the (second) downfall of Deng Xiaoping—an event which Cambodia was almost alone in welcoming.

The purge of the 'Gang of Four' in October that year must have come as something of a shock to Pol Pot, and the rise of Deng to his third life in power as an even more threatening development. The initial decision to reinstate Deng came in March 1977 (according to his semi-official biography). This coincided with a major purge in the Phnom Penh government, in which prominent leaders disappeared, presumed shot, including Hu Nim, who was the first to greet Sihanouk when the Prince set foot on liberated soil in 1973*. Could Hu Nim and the others have favoured a domestic line closer to Deng's 'four modernizations'? If Pol Pot purged his colleagues to protect his own policies, he certainly consolidated a social regime that ran completely counter to the new Chinese approach. To compensate, Pol Pot seems to have escalated the conflict with Vietnam, in order to retain the vital aid of Cambodia's only ally. As Hu Nim disappeared, Vietnam was denounced as an enemy and attacked. The Peking leadership was thereby trapped into supporting a government in Phnom Penh that became increasingly intolerable to Hanoi. Later, China's Ambassador to Laos predicted with approval a 'long, long war' between Vietnam and Cambodia.

If the Peking leadership had been more secure they would surely have done more to avoid such a risky course. But in early 1977 the Chinese Politbureau was deeply divided. Deng was only in the first stage of a comeback that threatened more than one member of the ruling 'group', and none was willing to risk his position by contradicting Maoist policy on an issue such as this. Thus the two weak and divided governments of Phnom Penh and Peking became locked into their disastrous course.

As the Cambodian leadership placed itself on a military footing in June 1977, Vietnam's General Giap went to China, for a tour of two or three weeks. A month later he gave the keynote speech to a Vietnamese Army conference on economic construction. His theme was the need for rapid industrialisation, but his ending

---

* For an account of Hu Nim's confession under torture in Pol Pot's prison, see p.117

These two photographs are on display in the streets of Hanoi: left, the famous picture of an American GI captured by a woman of the Vietcong; right, a Chinese soldier takes his place.

had a more ominous note: 'Some comrades believe that because we defeated the Americans no other enemy would dare touch us'. Such thinking was erroneous, he went on, and they should remain on their guard: 'If an aggressive war occurs in the future, our enemy will very possibly have a larger number of troops and more modern weapons than before'. This can hardly have been a reference to Democratic Kampuchea.

In September 1977, the forthcoming visit of Pol Pot to Peking was announced and it was made public for the first time that Cambodia was run by a Communist Party, with Pol Pot as its General Secretary. To celebrate the occasion another attack was apparently made against Vietnam. The Cambodian leader's lengthy visit to China was followed by a briefer one from Le Duan, ending on 25 November 1977. The next day the Hanoi government announced, with reference to Sino-Vietnamese relations: 'We will do our best to make this great friendship last forever'. In response, although without actually mentioning Vietnam by name, Peking defended its seizure of the Paracels, insisted that the Spratly islands belonged to China (and were therefore the object of Vietnamese aggression) and concluded, after having so defined itself as being attacked, with the threat: 'China will never attack first, but when it is attacked it will certainly counter-attack'.

By the end of December Vietnam had itself counter-attacked Cambodia. Receiving stiff resistance from the Khmer forces, which evidently surprised and impressed them, the Vietnamese made their peace offer of February 1978. When that failed so too did the 'moderate' policy Hanoi had pursued since 1975. Within weeks the vital rice trade of the South was nationalised, to prevent further speculation under conditions of war and terrible harvests (which were primarily a result of natural catastrophes). This move mainly affected the Chinese bourgeoisie of Cholon, who controlled the merchant networks of the South and who were soon to become 'boat people'.

The nationalisation measures signalled to Peking Vietnam's determination not to submit. Relations between the two countries degenerated rapidly. As Hanoi's dispositions for its full scale move into Cambodia became evident, China very nearly went to war, in the summer, to pre-empt the attack and thus preserve its uncomfortable ally. A decision was taken instead not to intervene directly, but to try to bog down the Vietnamese forces in a 'people's war' inside Cambodia.

Why Deng, having written off Democratic Kampuchea, should have decided upon the Vietnamese adventure is still somewhat mysterious. National pride is hardly the best reason for assaulting other countries and it could well be that internal politics were also a contributing factor. Wang Tung-hsing, Deng's major opponent in Peking, was the last and most senior Chinese leader to visit Cambodia. He came under fire in the wall-poster campaign Deng organised to strengthen his supremacy in November 1978. But he was not purged, and Deng may have feared that the humiliation suffered by China in Cambodia would be used against him in the future. Further speculation is out of place.

Recently, *Peking Review* accused Vietnam of 'bullying' China. Vietnam has enumerated 2,158 cases of Chinese harassment since 1974 of which 1,355 were by armed patrols (and we know from the Vietnam war that Hanoi's claims, when enumerated, are relatively accurate). Since Hanoi wanted its Chinese aid, it seems no more likely than that it was 'bullying' the United States in 1965. On the contrary, Vietnam feels itself beseiged by the Chinese regime. It went across the Cambodia border not in order to impose an Indochinese Federation, but rather to defend its flank. Obviously, Vietnamese troops should withdraw from Khmer territory when the attacks mounted from Thailand cease. But those who, like the US President, wish to demand such a retreat now should look also to the South China Sea. This is the site of China's real war claims.

Peking continues to insist that it will 'brook no incursion on China's sacred territory'—which implies all too clearly that it may seize the Spratly islands and destroy any oil rigs emplaced by the Vietnamese. The Harrier jump jets, which our own Industry Minister is busy trying to sell in Peking this week, are ideally suited to island warfare and will no doubt be 'defending' China's claims in the near future. While China maintains this position, it is obvious that Vietnam will never allow hostile MiGs to be based in Cambodia.

Who can look at the map of Chinese claims and regard Vietnam as the 'expansionist' power of Southeast Asia, and China's invasion as a response to this? Apparently the United States and British governments are able to do so. The verbal attack on Vietnam as an 'Asian Cuba' was launched with the acquiescence of Brzezinski. Now, an invasion has been mounted after Deng's return from the USA where, according to a *Washington Post* editorial, he was reassured that any 'punishment' he inflicted upon Vietnam would not disrupt the new alliance. China is not responding to events in Cambodia nor to Vietnamese 'bullying'. In effect, China is punishing Vietnam for its victory over the United States in 1975.

(23 February 1979)

The 'boat people' and the US blockade
John Pilger

While travelling in South-East Asia during the summer of 1979, I read the
following news items. One: Manilla police believe that America's Vietnam war
movie *The Deer Hunter* has directly inspired a spate of Russian-roulette killings in
the Philippines. 'The youths dress up like Americans', said a policeman, 'put a
single round in a revolver, and dare each other... the movie is real popular here.'

Two: President Carter saw his favourite movie, *The Deer Hunter,* for the third
time. He is reported to be 'deeply moved' by it, and comments on its 'authentic
American message'.

Three: Vietnam, threatened by famine in seven provinces, has again appealed
to the United States to 'forget the past and normalise relations, without conditions'. State Department sources said the President had no wish to recognise
Vietnam 'until decency takes root in that land... the kind of decency we understand in America'.

In another article, reprinted on p.30, I describe *The Deer Hunter*, that famous
Hollywood smash, as a lie which was designed to appease a sulking American
bitterness called 'the new patriotism'; to satiate the box-office demand for gratuitous violence; and to portray the Vietnamese as venal sub-humans, and the
Americans in Vietnam as tragic heroes. It was greeted by millions of Americans as
a mighty purgative for everything the Americans did in Vietnam. Today *The Deer
Hunter* is no longer a lie; it is a policy. And the policy is revenge.

This is revenge based on the need to punish the Vietnamese for daring to evict
the greatest military force in history. The policy is one which the President, the
American government, and the accessories to the American disaster in Vietnam—
such as Britain—now embrace with relish. Their cover is outrage in the name of
the boat people. Their prize is capital investment in, and trade with, the most
populous nation, China. Their aim is to justify the American war, and give
credence to other, similar adventures, and their delight is the spectacle of Vietnam
in isolation, an 'international pariah', struggling once again to live and to be heard.
It is as if we are watching the news films in reverse, and being returned with
indifference to the point of departure—as though no bombs were dropped, no
towns destroyed, no tears wept, no lessons learned.

Nothing, it seems, is to be allowed for the fact that the Vietnamese—exhausted and pauperised, with much of their land converted into a poisonous moonscape after thirty years of foreign vandalism—are once again a nation at war. This time the enemy is less visible than the French guns at Dien Bien Phu, the B-52s over Hanoi and Haiphong, the Chinese buglers leading the assault last February. Now it is an international campaign: not just to discredit, but to blockade and to starve. 'It may take five or ten years to crack their leadership', says a State Department man, 'but we'll do it'.

They will not, of course, 'do it' any more than they could do it at Khe Sanh or Hamburger Hill: any more than they could find the light in the endless metaphoric tunnel. But what they *are* doing is wounding again a people who more than any other have earned the right to some kind of peace.

The subterfuge of concern for the boat people has added a new dimension to an American blockade of Vietnam which has been in force since 1964: the 'food weapon', which Mrs Thatcher prefers to call, simply, 'pressure'. During journeys in Vietnam since the American departure, I have seen the results. In the northern province of Vinh, perhaps the most-bombed piece of this planet—which few Westerners have seen—the craters are so numerous and large that they join together, and not even the foundations of buildings remain.

Here people are living under straw, and among the children are the familiar veined faces, pot bellies and pencil limbs of acute malnutrition. Natural disaster has been added: two crops failed almost completely in 1976 and 1977, and in September last year the typhoons came early, producing the worst floods of the century, destroying three million tons of rice and a quarter of the country's livestock. Six million people were made homeless and malaria returned in its lethal cerebral form. A mission of American doctors and nutritionists sent by Senator Edward Kennedy's Committee to Vietnam expressed 'shock' at the condition of the people they saw, and appealed for the world to 'bring Vietnam back from the precipice of calamity'. There was minimal response to this.

At the peak of the food shortages, which made few headlines in the West, 600,000 Chinese troops—more than the Americans ever had in Vietnam—invaded without warning. They destroyed dykes and canals that had withstood Chinese invasions for 2,000 years, and American bombing more recently. They systematically blew up the last reserve stocks of rice, having been led to the food dumps by scouts recruited from among the *Hoa*, the ethnic Chinese of Vietnam.

The 'food weapon' was also wielded by Henry Kissinger, who created a 'zap office' in the State Department. Its task was to monitor the voting patterns of Third World countries, and to recommend 'zapping'—the suspension of food aid—for voting against US interests. During Kissinger's tenure, America gave more food aid to the Saigon regime than to any other country. This stopped abruptly in 1975. The new Vietnam was 'zapped'.

Kissinger's policy has been continued faithfully by President Carter, who has power to end the embargo without Congressional approval. Last autumn, with much of Vietnam still under water, the Kennedy mission appealed to the President to lift the embargo and 'save thousands of Vietnamese men, women and children by a single act of magnanimity.' He refused. Britain has now suspended aid to Vietnam, the bulk of which was to be £4 million worth of food. On 3 July the EEC, roused by Mrs Thatcher's 'humanitarian initiative' on behalf of the boat people, halted the shipment of 100,000 tons of food to Vietnam, which included 15,000 tons of skimmed milk for young children. 'One of the things that struck me',

reported a member of the Kennedy mission, 'was that milk powder for young children is what they desperately need.'

The tragedy of the boat people, now held to justify all this punishment, is the product of America's racist war against Vietnam, of China's most recent effort to subdue the Vietnamese, and of a state of siege in Hanoi and a despair that is like a presence.

Most of the first wave of refugees were the 'Cholon Chinese' of Saigon, who controlled the mosaic of corruption that was the South Vietnamese economy. The richest of them flew away with their gold before the collapse of April 1975, but the rest continued to control the Mekong rice trade for *three years* under the Hanoi government. In March 1978, their businesses were nationalised—not out of racial spite, or even political dogma, but largely because southern Vietnam was under attack from the Pol Pot regime in Cambodia, backed by 10,000 Chinese 'advisers'. There was no alternative but to impose the wartime rationing long accepted in the North.

If there was a racial distinction, it was drawn by the Peking government which insisted that the Chinese of Vietnam were not Vietnamese at all, but 'people of the motherland'. At the same time, Peking exhorted them to flee—which they did. That the new Vietnamese authorities, mostly at the level of the *To* (the neighbourhood committee) extracted their pound of flesh in terms of gold and property is beyond doubt. But what is also beyond doubt is that the Hanoi government, unavailingly, gave Peking the opportunity to mount an orderly evacuation of its 'nationals'.

Despite thirty years of war, of attacks from Cambodia, of threats from China, there has been no wholesale revenge in Vietnam: no 'rivers of blood'. Since the end of the American war, I have been to Saigon, and met openly people I knew well before: middle-class and capitalist to the core. Their misery is that of the harsh economic times they share with most of the population, though their prospects—often of life in the food-producing 'new economic zones'—are indeed something for which nothing in their former life prepared them. Their predicament is to have become the flotsam of the greatest consumer society in the world that produced little except dollar millionaires, Coke and drug addicts. When the Americans left, and pulled the intravenous tubes which fed that society, their own creation, they left these people with nothing, except a desire to follow.

The ethnic Chinese of the north are very different. They were mostly skilled workers who had blended with Vietnamese society, and were vital to the northern economy: so much so that after 1975, and during the Chinese campaign against 'racial persecution' in Vietnam, the Hanoi government offered them economic incentives.

That changed abruptly when the Chinese army attacked, and it was found that *Hoa* scouts had led the Chinese commandos around the mountain passes. The anger felt by this betrayal rebounded unjustly on all ethnic Chinese in the North who found themselves singled out as pawns in a struggle between their homeland and their 'motherland'. On the one side, Chinese troops killed those who refused to collaborate. On the other, the Vietnamese gave them the choice of crossing into China, or of going to the new economic zones—far from the northern frontier, and far from the eastern coast where the next Chinese invasion is expected. The third option was the sea voyage to Hong Kong.

These choices were brutal, and cannot in any way be condoned. But there must be some account of the circumstances which produced them.

No doubt headlines like 'An Asian Holocaust'—taken up by a half-page *Guardian* advertisement in July 1979, paid for by a group of leading British charities—will get the postal orders flowing in. And certainly the refugees crushed behind the high wire fences in Hong Kong need help. But to compare the boat people with the Jews of the Holocaust is to profane the memory of those who were led to the gas chambers of Auschwitz. Oxfam is one of the signatories to the *Guardian* advertisement: Oxfam's director, Brian Walker, was in Vietnam in January 1978, and returned with only words of sympathy and understanding for the country's dreadful post-war problems, and measured praise for 'considerable strides in human rights'. He made no allusion to a 'Holocaust' then.

The campaign to equate Vietnam with Nazi Germany involves some inexcusable omissions. No mention is made of the Vietnamese request to Washington to fly out 10,000 refugees a month in an 'airbridge' similar to that which operated between Havana and Miami through the 60's and which ensured that 700,000 people left Cuba without a single loss of life.

The Vietnamese government and the UN High Commissioner for Refugees have agreed on a plan to fly out ethnic Chinese. But the catch, of course, is that people cannot leave if no country will take them. Nor has there been mention of the 320,000 Cambodian refugees—as many as all the boat people—who were given refuge in Vietnam from a genuine holocaust, produced by the Cambodian regime of Pol Pot, which perhaps exterminated a quarter of the Khmer population. How many charity advertisements were there on behalf of these people?

The paramount tragedy, for the Vietnamese and for the boat people, is the repulse of Vietnam's unrelenting—even pathetic—attempts at conciliation with America. For more than a year before Washington gave its blessing to the Chinese invasion (and President Carter renewed the economic embargo) Vietnam had dropped all claims to the $3.4 billion reparations promised in the Paris accords of 1972. The Vietnamese invited a conga line of American bankers, oilmen, travel agents and Congressmen to Hanoi to discuss business, investment, tourism and diplomatic recognition. When I was there in the summer of 1978, they moved a Cuban delegation out of the best hotel to make way for some bankers from the Chase Manhattan. Most of these initiatives were the work of Nguyen Co Thach, the Secretary of State for Foreign Affairs, who said this in June 1979 to a visiting group from the American Chamber of Commerce of Hong Kong.

On 29 September last year, after months of talks, I met Richard Holbrooke (US Assistant Secretary of State) in New York. We accepted the US position on normalisation. We agreed to defer other problems until later. We agreed on the number of embassy staff, even where the embassies would be located. *Everything* was agreed. I waited in New York through October and then I had to go home. In November I got a message that there was now 'a question of Cambodia'.

The old Deer Hunters in Washington not only encouraged the Chinese to attack Vietnam (what became of John Foster Dulles' 'campaign to save the brave peoples of Vietnam and Southeast Asia from the evils of Chinese Communism'?) They also condemned Vietnam for invading Cambodia and overthrowing the genocidal regime of Pol Pot. Speaking last month, Thach repeated that from Vietnam's side normalisation was still available without conditions. He added that with relations once established, 'anything' would be possible. Vietnam would even consider requests for US ships and planes 'to use our facilities, provided they respect our sovereignty'. Asked to recall the American war, he said: 'I would rather not talk about it... I don't want to open the past.'

This is not just conciliation towards a former enemy: Thach's words reflect a desperate wish to extricate Vietnam from the cold war between Russia and China. Hoping that America would respond, the Vietnamese held off signing a 'friendship treaty' with the Russians, whose assistance they have never used except with a long-handled spoon. Only when the State Department tried to stop World Bank grants to Vietnam did they reluctantly join Comecon. They are now charged with being in peonage to Moscow. This is not true, but the isolation now imposed on them is apt to produce that very condition.

Of course, the cynicism directed at Vietnam is extended to the boat people. No government, least of all the British, is giving refuge to people because they are helpless. There is no orderly queue in the camps of Hong Kong. There is, in the words of a UN camp supervisor, 'nothing more than a human meat market and a buyer's market at that'.

America has five strict categories in its 'Indochinese Parole Programme.' If you are a former CIA runner, you make it. If you are an illiterate fisherman you are Category Five and do not make it. One day last week there were 61,144 refugees in Hong Kong. On the same day, *one* refugee 'qualified' for re-settlement in the West.

Meanwhile, the President of the United States remains 'deeply moved' by *The Deer Hunter,* and deaf to the pleas of an exhausted and hungry nation. That his country's war caused the death and maiming of several million Vietnamese, and the flight of countless refugees on land and sea, and achieved *nothing,* in the cause of *nothing,* is the saddest truth of my time. That so many appear to have forgotten this, or do not wish to remember, or do not care, is a great pity. That vengeance should be visited on a peasant people, because they had the effrontery to win their independence, is a crime.

(20 July 1979)

Why the Deer Hunter is a lie
John Pilger

Eleven years ago I went to the movies in Montgomery, Alabama. It was a Saturday night and the local fleapalace was packed, mostly with 'good ole boys' who, in those days, hung about gas stations and giggled menacingly at the occupants of any car with out-of-Dixie plates. This was the summer of 1968; children had died in the firebombing of a black church in Montgomery, Richard Nixon was making his comeback and the American war in Vietnam was at its peak. The movie was *The Green Berets*, starring John Wayne.

From scene one they cheered. They threw their beer cans and yelped and when 'The Duke' dealt single-handedly with an entire regiment of gooks, a Buddha shape in front of me, hoarse with adulation, stood and saluted.

Like a fool, I laughed through it all, and therefore found myself having to exit well before the credits, and smartly. It didn't matter that I knew Vietnam and the war; this was such a *bad* movie—badly put together, badly acted—and so unwittingly silly that it was funny. And although it was hailed in towns like Montgomery, where John Wayne is part of the weaning process, it was generally dismissed as crude Hollywood stuff, whose antics by no stretch of the imagination tallied with the nightly television images of napalmed civilians and the greatest military machine in history going nowhere.

The other night I saw *The Deer Hunter*, which, as almost everybody must know by now, is about Vietnam, plus nice pictures of small-town America, a wedding and mountains. This film has been nominated for so many awards that only the Congressional Medal of Honour appears to be missing and the bestowal of that appropriate gong might well be a possibility if the relentless eulogising continues, here and in America. So finely orchestrated has been the pre-publicity for this film that 'Have you seen *The Deer Hunter*?' has become a breathless catch cry of one-upmanship. Indeed, it is difficult to get seats for a film which Derek Malcolm in *The Guardian* insists we should see 'at all costs', and which the *Daily Mail* describes as 'the story they never dared to tell before... the film that could purge a nation's guilt!' and which left Milton Shulman 'quivering and shattered' and which, according to Alexander Walker in the *Evening Standard*, 'says things that needed saying'. And so on, and so on. Lady Delfont, wife of one of the backers apparently wept openly.

There is much to weep about. The backers and makers of this film are reported to have spent fourteen million dollars on sifting the ashes of one of history's most documented atrocities—in order to re-package it and re-sell it as a Hollywood 'smash' that will, and probably already has, made them fortunes; to reincarnate the triumphant Batman-jawed Caucasian warrior and to present a suffering, courageous people as sub-human Oriental brutes and dolts; to convert truth into lie. And, as I say, if the queues and touts at the box office are any indication, they are getting away with it.

Compared with *The Deer Hunter*, *The Green Berets* was an honest film; its B-movie fantasy was discernible to all but the most evangelical 'patriot'. *The Deer Hunter* is technically slick, and perhaps its documentary and *verité* effects are even brilliant; *something* must have prompted usually discriminating critics to opt for unction and naïvete.

And, I suppose, for those who have forgotten what Vietnam was really about, or would wish to forget, or are too young to remember, or are truly naïve, the slickness is persuasive; the wedding guests act like wedding guests, the blood gushes, the bullets thud and the rotors of helicopters make the sound that is forever embedded in my brain, from years of attending the reality. Otherwise, the symbolism is leaden (one shot for the proud stag etc.) the *schmaltz* elongated and the sadism utterly gratuitous: the kind of sadism that packs 'em in.

There are times when, even by the film's own standards, the slick runs precariously thin; the strong, silent Batman-jawed Robert DeNiro and the brave, sensitive, baby-faced Boy Wonder Christopher Walken could not merely suffer in captivity as soldiers; no, the Dynamic Duo get away by wiping out a house-full of their barbaric captors, mighty M-16s rotating from their hips. Pow! Wham! Rat-tat-tat! 'C'mon, letzgetouttahere!' *ad nauseam*. Big John would have shown them how it's really done.

This is how Hollywood created the myth of the Wild West, which was harmless enough unless you happened to be an American Indian, and how World War Two and the Korean War were absorbed into box office folklore, which was harmless enough unless you happened to be a dumb Kraut or an unspeakable Nip or a Commie chink, or one of a malleable generation and liable to be conditioned by endless, bragging, simplistic good guy/bad guy images of war. And of course, *The Deer Hunter* is harmless enough unless you happen to be a gook, Commie or otherwise, or of a generation too young to remember genocidal 'free fire zones' and towns and villages that 'had to be destroyed to save them'.

That the same cynical mythmaking is now being applied to Vietnam (there'll be *Deer Hunter 2*, I bet) induces more melancholy than anger in those like myself, who saw whole Vietnamese communities used as guinea pigs for the testing of a range of 'anti-personnel' military technology, and who saw demoralised, brutalised, often mutinous and doped American teenagers lying in their own blood and shit, for the purposes of some pointless, sacrificial siege staged in the cause of nothing, except the gratification of inept brass in their air-conditioned bubbles.

There is not a passing hint in *The Deer Hunter* that Vietnam was, above all, a war of rampant technology against human beings. There are, however, heavenly violins.

Richard Grenier, the New York critic, tells me that the director of *The Deer Hunter*, Michael Cimino, is being hailed in America as the champion of the 'new patriotism'. Linda Christmas of the *Guardian* reported Cimino as saying

> During the making of the film, I certainly had a sense that we were doing something special. It was such an agonising experience both emotionally, physically—the tropics, the heat, the humidity. I can't shake off *The Deer Hunter* even now. I have this insane feeling that I was there, in Vietnam. Somehow the fine wires have got really crossed and the line between reality and fiction has become blurred.

The above is how you 'sell' and justify a myth. Cimino is an expert salesman. He sold *The Deer Hunter* without a script. Originally, it was to be the recollections of a group of former GIs, but what helped to convince the major backers that they were on to a winner were the orgiastic Russian roulette scenes that recur throughout the film and leave an audience with the impression that the Vietnamese gamble on human life as casually as the British gamble on the pools.

How odd: in Vietnam, I never heard about this game. I have asked other correspondents and they have never heard about this game. And interviews with POWs never mentioned this game; but much of Cimino's picture is given over to this 'meaningful horror', which he insists happened and which is meant to be somehow redemptive.

There is another problem. Although Cimino says he has 'this insane feeling that I was there, in Vietnam', he was never there. He told Linda Christmas, and Leticia Kent of the *New York Times,* that he was called up shortly after the *Tet* offensive in 1968 and was a medic attached to the Green Berets. He 'missed' Vietnam because, he says, he had a job 'involved in defence and classified. Something to do with that...'

The Pentagon's records tell a different story. He was in the army reserve before draftees were sent to Vietnam and was pursuing a career in advertising at the time of *Tet*. These minor discrepancies would matter little, except that they may help to explain something about the source of *The Deer Hunter's* mythmaking.

The timing of *The Deer Hunter* is perfect. The 'new patriotism' and the mood of national redemption decree that it is time the American conscience was salved and the Vietnamese 'punished' for defeating and humiliating the greatest power on earth. In February 1979, Vietnam was attacked by America's new ally, China, on the pretext that the Vietnamese were the stooges of Moscow. The American Government condemned the Chinese action with all the force of a verbal leg-slap, while linking it, astutely, to a condemnation of Hanoi's overthrow of the genocidal regime in Cambodia; there was no mention that Cambodia had attacked Vietnam in 1977.

During these past weeks of 'punishment'—when the Vietnamese, by most accounts, stopped their latest invader—official Washington statements neglected to mention that the Vietnamese had been pleading for diplomatic ties with America with such desperation that they had dropped all previous demands for reparations; that for two years the Vietnamese, having maintained their independence from both Russia and China during the war years, had resisted Russian pressure to sign a 'friendship treaty', until they had no choice; that the Americans ignored these overtures and used their influence to prevent Asian Development Bank funds going to Vietnam for desperately needed reconstruction aid.

And who now is vocal in backing China's 'punishment' of Vietnam, and China's ambition to 'smash the myth of Vietnam's invincibility'? William C. Westmoreland, one of the chief architects of American vandalism (and defeat) in Vietnam;

Senator John Tower, hero of the far right; Nguyen Ky, former President of South Vietnam (now in the liquor business in California); patriots all.

I was in Vietnam last year. It seems incredible that there is still need to offer reminders of what was done to that nation. But, with Hollywood now re-making history, and with current events being reported so as to make the Vietnamese appear as Oriental Prussians, such reminders are necessary.

Much of North Vietnam is a moonscape, from which visible signs of life—houses, factories, schools, hospitals, pagodas, churches—have been obliterated.* Forty-four per cent of the forests have been destroyed; in many of those still standing there are no longer birds and animals; and there are lorry drivers who will not respond to the hooting of a horn because they are deaf from the incessant sound of bombs; and there are some 30,000 children in Hanoi and Haiphong alone who are permanently deaf as a result of the American bombing at Christmas 1972.

The B52s spared the spacious French-built centre of the cities and laid 'carpets' of bombs down such crowded arteries as Kham Thiem Street in Hanoi, where today an old nicotine-stained figure with a wispy beard keeps a vigil at a gap where 283 people died. 'It was a block of flats', he told me, 'we were mostly the old, women and children. There was no time to reach the shelters, and we sang as the bombs came down... singing is louder than bombs'. Such dignity, out of horror, is representative of the Vietnamese and differs sharply from Mr Cimino's fantasies. (More bombs were dropped on Vietnam than ever dropped during all of World War Two and Korea combined: the greatest aerial onslaught ever.)

In Hanoi's Bach Mai Hospital, doctors have discovered that 'Napalm B', which

From 'The Deer Hunter'.

the Dow Chemical Company created especially for Vietnam, continues to smoulder under the skin's tissues through the lifetime of its victims. People continue to die from the effects of plastic needles which were sprayed by bombs created especially for Vietnam and designed so that the needles moved through human organs and escape detection, even under X-ray.

Places called Ham Long and Dong Loc ought to be as well known as Dresden, but they are not. Ham Long, like so many towns in the north, was bombed literally back to the Stone Age: every day for four years, from five in the morning till two in the afternoon, the planes came in low from carriers in the South China Sea. At Cu Chi, in the south, an horizon that was once thick vegetation now shimmers in the heat, laid completely to waste 'for maybe half a century or more', according to the report of one member of an American Academy of Science team. This is the result of 'Operation Hades' (later Hollywoodised to 'Operation Ranch Hand'): the defoliation and poisoning of the landscape and crops, and the sowing of the seeds of human mutations for generations. In 1970 I wrote about a 'foetal disaster' at the Tu Duc Hospital in Saigon where deformed babies were beginning to arrive by the dozen: the result, said American doctors at the time, of an aerial spray called 245-T, which is banned in the United States.

That is enough, I suppose. There are the tens of thousands of heroin addicts, and a strain of VD for which there is no certain cure. There are the permanently dislocated and the insane, who ran from General Westmoreland's 'free fire zones'. And there are the thousands of American-fathered children; several of them were singing a song when I visited a Saigon orphanage. I wrote these words in the *New Statesman* in 1978 and I believe they are worth repeating. 'The war is gone... planes come no more... do not weep for those just born... the human being is evergreen'. If you see *The Deer Hunter*, you may like to remember these lines.

Next week, General Westmoreland arrives in Britain to publicise an illustrated history of the Vietnam war. Its 550 photographs are principally concerned with American tanks, helicopters, planes, artillery and other weapons in spectacular action. Its section on 'The Air War against North Vietnam' makes no reference to civilian casualties. General Westmoreland's foreword is, apparently, 'a hard-hitting comment on the effect of political influences on the military performance of the anti-Communist forces'.

(16 March 1979)

Wouldn't hurt a mouse
Mike Goldwater and
Anthony Barnett

In a modestly equipped hospital, short of drugs, Le Hu Thin strove to end a difficult confinement. She wanted a son. But it was immediately evident that her baby was deformed—almost beyond recognition as a human infant. It was a boy, but he had anencephalia: he was without a brain.

He lived for 28 hours, from 20 September 1979 until the next day when his body was preserved in formaldehyde for medical history. After two miscarriages, he had been his parents' first child. In poor, predominantly rural countries, there are many miscarriages, and a greater number of seriously defective babies than in the West. But this baby's deformity was more than usually severe.

His father, Nguyen Van Oans, had been a driver on the Ho Chi Minh trail, hundreds of miles to the south of the family's home. In order to deprive the drivers of cover, the United States defoliated the area of the trails with Agent Orange, the colloquial name for the herbicide 245-T which has as its contaminant dioxin. To this day, the manufacturers, Dow Chemicals, claim that it poses no risk to users. But there is little doubt that it harms those on whom it is used. Dioxin is known to be a teratogen, to cause birth deformities.

Le Hu Thin has never been to the South; nor did she have contact with any chemical products before or during her pregnancy. Her husband, Oans, was sprayed three times with Agent Orange.

In a way, they are lucky that their child is dead. Quyen is four. She has microcephalia, which means that her brain is smaller than a monkey's. She cries, is hyperactive, then sleeps briefly, then cries again—in quick rotation, day and night. Her mother, Phung Thi Ngo, 25, has always lived in her northern village, and in a careful survey medical researchers found no history of birth defects in the entire 'greater family' of more than 100 people. Quyen's father, Nguyen Van Quach, 35, fought in the South and was sprayed many times. Doctors confirm that his sperm is abnormal. Asked if any of his friends from the army also had deformed children he replied that of the 92 men in his basic unit, he was the only survivor. However, he had a friend from another unit who had survived. This man had been sprayed on many occasions: his first child was born with anencephalia, his second with only one arm and his third with only two toes.

Phung Thi Ngo is now pregnant again and the baby is due at the end of the year.

Mike Goldwater (Network)

Bui Van Xuan is 20 months old and was born without eyes. His father is 28 and is a veteran soldier from the liberation army in the south of Vietnam. He was sprayed three times with Agent Orange. Xuan cannot speak or stand up. Xuan's mother, Pham Thi Huan is 24. This child is her first. She is now pregnant again. The family live in a small village, My An, in the province of Hai Hung.

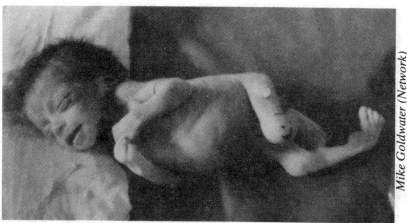

Mike Goldwater (Network)

Pham Xuan Lo was born on 10 June 1980. He was two weeks old and in an oxygen tent when this photograph was taken at the Institute for the Care of Mother and Child in Hanoi. Lo's father was sprayed while a soldier in the south, and he is still in the army. He is 35 years old and his wife is 28. She works in a post office in a suburb of Hanoi. Lo is their first child. He has deformed hands and feet, was born prematurely and weighs 1.6 kgms. The doctors at the hospital thought he had several other internal malformations and could not intervene. They only expected Lo to live for one more week.

If this too is deformed, it will seem to the villagers that the family has been cursed. Those who have been mutilated by war get an allowance, but a family with only helpless young mouths is a further burden to a community which has already little enough.

The same fear dogs Pham Thi Huan, who is 24 and half way through her second pregnancy. Her first child, Bui Van Xuan, is 20 months old. He can neither speak nor stand up and he suffers from anophtalmia: he has no eyes. His father, Bui Van Tram, 28, is a veteran soldier from the Liberation army and was sprayed three times with Agent Orange, between 1971 and 1974.

Vu Thi Lam and her husband Dam Viet Thyoc are luckier: they have three lively and intelligent daughters, all able to work. The eldest, now 16, was born just before President Johnson ordered the full scale American intervention in Vietnam. A normal, self-conscious teenager, she refused to be photographed. Her young sisters, Lien, eight, and Hien, six, did not object to such attention. They were born after Dam Viet Thuoc went South and was sprayed, and neither has lenses in her eyes. But they have each other, and blindness has improved their linguistic memories. With special attention, they will still be able to make something of their lives.

Nobody has any idea how many other children suffer equivalent defects throughout Vietnam. Nor does anybody know how many generations will be affected. Where chromosome damage in a parent leads to deformity in a child, will that child carry the same reproducing wound? If a man with sperm that is, say 40 per cent damaged is fortunate to sire a healthy child, will the child unwittingly carry genetic damage into the next generation?

Chloracne, which is a severe skin eruption, is one of the more immediate and

Mike Goldwater (Network)

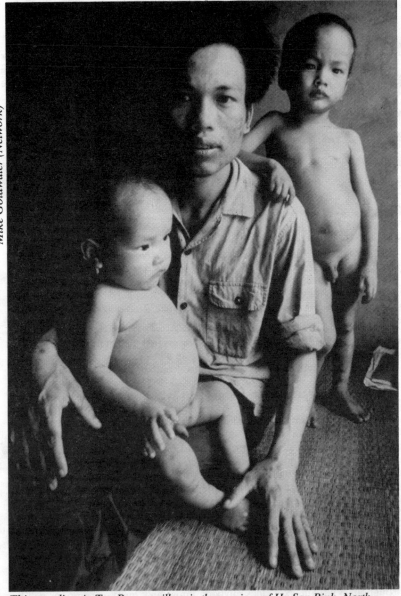

This man lives in Tan Peuong village in the province of Hu Son Binh, North
Vietnam. As a soldier on the Ho Chi Minh Trail, he was sprayed directly with Agent
Orange. His two sons both have heart defects.

'less serious manifestations of dioxin exposure', according to an American research team. There was an outbreak of chloracne among the people of Seveso in north Italy, when a chemical plant exploded in 1976, releasing a cloud of dioxin. In Vietnam, a man who suffered from severe chloracne after being sprayed on the Ho Chi Minh trail and in Laos, still has serious attacks of it today. His two young sons, born since the war, also suffer from it—as well as having heart defects. 'I don't understand why the child also has chloracne', comments Hanoi Professor Ton Duc Lang. 'We have never seen this before.'

Of the 17 million gallons of herbicide dropped on Vietnam, (which poisoned ten per cent of its main forests, more than a third of its mangrove forests and three per cent of its cultivated land) more than 11 million gallons were Agent Orange. It is not yet understood just how it has affected the food chain of field, fish and animals.

Vietnam has neither the medical nor the statistical services to cope with the consequences, or even adequately to measure them. In Hanoi, a group of able and distinguished doctors, led by Professors Lang, Tung, Van and Tuyen, are busy conducting investigations. They found the children described here (and many, many more) and arranged for them to be photographed. But Hanoi was far removed from the sprayed regions and to the South, unfortunately, no equivalent work is being done. In central Vietnam, where the country narrows and the trails and mountains meet the sea, there are villages below the slopes which draw on the waters of poisoned ranges. To the north-west of Saigon, the Tay Ninh region was repeatedly sprayed: in the main hospital there, *one quarter* of all births are miscarriages. Seven thousand American GIs who came into contact with Agent Orange are suing for massive sums. By contrast, the Vietnamese are asking not for compensation, but only for help to investigate the damage done.

In April 1980, a delegation of six went to the White House in Washington with a petition which requested the US government to recognise Hanoi and acknowledge the need for humanitarian assistance to be sent there. They met Roger Sullivan of the US National Security Council, who has this to say: 'To put it in terms of a Chinese dialectic, United States policy is exactly to squeeze Vietnam as hard as we can, to force Vietnam to rely on the Soviet Union: then Vietnam will find the Soviet Union cannot meet all its needs... If Vietnam suffers economic hardships, I think that is just great.'

A recent study by the US National Toxicology Programme is being presented as proof that Agent Orange does not cause reproductive problems in males. One hundred male mice were exposed to varying levels of 245-T, 24-D and dioxin (the components of Agent Orange). After 20 weeks, they were found to have lost weight and suffered changes in their thymus glands and livers which were 'primarily related' to dioxin, but otherwise they remained healthy. When mated after eight weeks, they did not differ from the control group in numbers of impregnations, still births, birth defects, or ratios of male to female offspring.

British expert on dioxin, Dr Alistair Hay of Leeds University, says these findings cannot be discounted, but points out that people in Vietnam may have been exposed to different concentrations of Agent Orange, and over longer periods of time. The defoliant is thought to have contained higher levels of dioxin earlier in the war than it did later on. And in any case, it is not certain that humans react to Agent Orange in the same way as mice.

(22 August 1980)

Part II
Kissinger and the historical record

The Pornography of Power

Bruce Page on The White House Years, 1968-1972
by Henry Kissinger

During the middle sixties at Harvard University, Government Course 180, *The Principles of International Relations,* was taught by Professor Henry Kissinger. He had made his name as a student of 19th-century diplomatic history, and added to it with studies of nuclear weaponry: although there was nothing to foreshadow his present-day eminence, he had some extra-academic standing as an adviser to the Rockefellers, and to the Kennedy and Johnson administrations.

Kissinger's discourse made a powerful impact upon some of his students. It began, as one of them recalls, from the notion that nuclear armouries made it difficult for Great Powers to graduate military threats in the way that they once supposedly did. Once. it had been possible for a Bismarck to notch up tension in Europe's chancelleries—gaining his way thereby—through issuing commands for mobilisation. But how to do this with nuclear missiles permanently mobilised, just a button-push away from 'mutual assured destruction'?

Such a situation, according to Kissinger, placed a 'significant premium' upon irrationality. The line of argument, says his ex-student ran like this:

> There is a clear element of power over your opponents if they can be persuaded to believe that excess zeal on your part might touch off nuclear war.
> This particular lecture made one of the clearest impressions of my Harvard years. It is trenchant stuff: but fraught with a veritable hall of mirrors of treble... quadruple... multiple think. And underlying it the sombre, but then unstated, requirement to acquire a record of irrational deeds.

Also, this student recalls Dr Kissinger saying, in so many words, that the requirement of irrationality was 'unfortunately... at odds with the democratic political system'. (True enough: Barry Goldwater's Presidential candidacy had just been wiped out because he was considered irrational on the question of nuclear warfare.) Therefore, Kissinger thought, totalitarian regimes had a powerful advantage in world affairs.

Practical people commonly assume that nonsense talked by academics and intellectuals has little impact upon the real world. But this case, at least, is not so simple. A few years later, at the outset of his star-crossed Presidency, Richard Nixon privately explained his conception of international relations to the White

House adviser H.R. (Bob) Haldeman. The story is told by William Shawcross in his book *Sideshow* (much anathematised by Dr Kissinger), and it is worth mentioning that it refers to a period when most respectable opinion portrayed the Nixon White House as a citadel of modest, conservative calm.

> He said, 'I call it the Madman Theory, Bob. I want the North Vietnamese to believe I've reached the point where I might do *anything* to stop the war. We'll just slip the word to them that "for God's sake, you know Nixon is obsessed about Communism. We can't restrain him when he's angry—and he has his finger on the nuclear button"—and Ho Chi Minh himself will be in Paris in two days begging for peace.'[1]

Where, and how, could Nixon have acquired such an idea? And once acquired, how sustained?

The question stares at us across a decade, and across several million corpses. For whatever the Seventies brought to Indochina, it was not peace. There had, of course, been great suffering there during the Sixties, and it was too much to hope it might end easily with the decade. But scarcely anyone can have imagined the Sixties as merely an overture to impending nightmares: an intensified war fought (despite the distribution of Nobel Peace Prizes) to its bitter conclusion; aerial bombardment like none seen before; famine, fresh wars (China versus Vietnam, Vietnam versus Cambodia); the expulsion of the Boat People; the ascendancy (still legally recognised by our country) of Pol Pot and his lethal automatons.

On one account, this catastrophe was due to a gigantic misuse of the power of America, still by vast margins the world's most richly-endowed nation. Shawcross's *Sideshow* is a chief document of any such indictment. On another, it was due precisely to an *insufficient* deployment of American power: that Indochina's misfortunes (mirrored elsewhere in the world) begin with the ambitions of totalitarian communism, and that the Western military resistance which is alone capable of checking those ambitions is systematically undermined by liberal guilt and by socialist collaboration. Dr Kissinger's huge memoir[2] is largely devoted to upholding this view: he claims that the architecture of his Indochina peace would have held, had not the US Congress foolishly stripped the Presidency of its ability to deploy air power and military assistance. Thus, the monstrous determination of the totalitarians prevailed. One cannot, he says, blame the nature of a regime upon those who, like himself, tried to resist it but were betrayed. He has the support of, among others, the *Wall Street Journal* and the *Economist* in drawing from this geopolitical conclusions extending far beyond Indochina: if such betrayals are not corrected in future, then our civilisation is doomed.

It is not so hard to show that Kissinger's account of American involvement in South-east Asia is a web of untruths—to an extent which makes *The White House Years* implausible as a witness to anything. It is less easy to understand why this should be so, to explain why a man of Kissinger's gifts feels he can proffer a view of the world which—for all its dress of sophistication—would be too crude for a

---

[1] *Sideshow* (André Deutsch), serialised NS 15, 22, 29 June 1979. Shawcross cites Haldeman and Di Mona, *The Ends of Power*, p.83.
[2] *The White House Years 1968-1972* by Henry Kissinger, Michael Joseph/ Weidenfeld 1979.

schoolchild equipped with any decent sense of curiosity. A notable example occurs at p. 518:

> It was Hanoi—animated by an insatiable drive to dominate Indochina—that... organised the Khmer Rouge long before *any* American bombs fell on Cambodia soil.

No. Anyone investigating the plausible-enough idea of a Vietnamese desire to colonise Cambodia discovers early on that the North Vietnamese maintained for many years their own cadres of Khmer communists. These were kept leashed in Hanoi during the long time that the North Vietnamese considered the 'neutralist' Cambodia regime of Prince Sihanouk to be a better option for them than a loyal, but dependent satellite. The Khmer Rouge, originally a fraction devoted to Sihanouk's overthrow, loathed Hanoi precisely because it offered no help against the Prince. After Sihanouk was replaced by the American client Lon Nol, the Vietnamese tried to take over (or supplant) the Khmer Rouge *maquis* by sending their own long-domesticated Cambodians down the Ho Chi Minh trail. Pol Pot's men slaughtered them. If the Khmer Rouge are seriously beholden to anybody, it is to the Chinese—whose Asian ambitions are scarcely smaller than Vietnam's,[3] but who appear in Kissinger's account as co-conspirators with himself for peace.

Naturally this interesting, if wretched reality must be collapsed in order to allow Kissinger to draw a straight, clear line of blame. Before going further into the structure of such boldly-made but feebly-based contentions, it helps to look at the nature of Kissinger's book, and the nature of his claim to rule.

Very spacious claims are made for *The White House Years*. The *Sunday Times*, which is serialising it at length, celebrates its 'style' and 'richness'. 'A stunning book,' says Thomas Bray of the *Wall Street Journal*, '... a major inquiry into the nature and art of statecraft... gem-like profiles of foreign leaders... Mr Kissinger's account of his secret trip to China shines.' Even a hostile critic like Stanley Hoffman in *The New York Review of Books* finds it intellectually impressive, and says that Kissinger, if not otherwise engaged, might have made a novelist of quality. Nonetheless, Hoffman reflects, there is something 'airless and oppressive' about the volume.

This does not go nearly far enough. Not only is the book, as a literary artefact, gruesomely bad: its badness is connected with its true nature as a work of propaganda, and connected somewhat with the undue deference which Kissinger continues to be paid. To begin quietly, here is a well-praised example of one of Kissinger's gems of portraiture (the subject being Edward Heath):

> He was not free of the complexes imposed by Britain's class history... The ruthlessness necessary to achieve his ambition did not come naturally and was all the more noticeable for that reason... He was a warm and gentle person who anticipated rejection and fended it off with a formal politeness (punctuated often with a laugh distinguished by its lack of mirth).

The result (surely leaving Tolstoy secure upon his pedestal) would be acceptable enough in a provincial newspaper obituary: it is supposed, however, to be one of the plums in Kissinger's enormous duff. It is surely unusual to read 1,500 pages of recollections by a professional intellectual, and find them practically devoid of

---

[3]See Anthony Barnett, 'The Chinese Invasion', p.19.

general cultural references: those that occur being apt to clang appallingly. During his 'shining' account of the Chinese expedition, Kissinger tells Chou En-Lai that some of his experiences make him feel like

> the plumber in Kafka's novel *The Castle,* who, having been summoned and then denied entrance, spent his life trying to get in...

Given the fate of the Nixon Administration, the substitution of 'plumber' may just be a hilarious Freudianism: but it's hard to believe that anyone who has really encountered that unbearable book could forget that 'K', the protagonist in *The Castle,* is a land-surveyor, for K's profession is woven into the tale almost as firmly as Shylock's into *The Merchant of Venice.*

An intellectual might be defined, negatively, as someone who tries not to mangle literature. Naturally, you can be a perfectly good cook, Pola navigator or surgeon without claiming intellectual virtues. But you may not be invited to Harvard to preach the Madman Theory of War, nor appointed in Washington to practise it.

Elsewhere, our cultivated statesman fondly re-invents the literary wheel. Reflecting that it's tough at the geopolitical top, he says:

> I read a novel once, based on the proposition that each human being has a finite amount of qualities like courage, and endurance and wisdom, and that life consists of expending these ever-dwindling resources.

This surely is not the only theme of literature but it's about the hardest to overlook: being established in the *Iliad* and the *Odyssey,* elaborated in the tale of Beowulf's final monster, and carried no doubt into the epics of cultures other than our own. The fact that in each individual case the contest betwen *virtu* and *fortuna* has just one result was pointed out to Roland before Roncesvalles, noted by Cassius of Portia's suicide, and defied by the horn outside the Dark Tower. Sweeney among the nightingales: all this comes down to something Kissinger picked up somewhere? (In a *Reader's Digest* version of *The Red Badge of Courage*?) The reader will not by now be amazed to learn that Cambodia's fate unfolds with (yes) 'all the inevitability of Greek tragedy': script by Henry Kissinger and Richard Nixon, based on an idea by Euripides.

Literature aside, one is surprised, not so much that a Professor of Government (and world statesman) should express total ignorance of economics, as by the aggressive incuriosity of Kissinger's approach to the subject. Much space is consumed in denouncing the 'moralistic' foreign-policy tradition of pre-Nixonian Washington, and its supposedly lamentable effect upon America's international potency. The idea that this falling-off might have something to do with the collapse of the dollar (due in good part to costly military adventuring) is not mentioned even by way of denial.

Still more curiously, there is an almost total absence of reference to the major texts on Kissinger's own subject: statecraft, its philosophy and history. One quick pat for Lord Bryce, an un-indexed nod to de Tocqueville's *Memoirs*—the reader, at this point, feels like one who, forcing down gelid cocoa, is reminded of the taste of chilled champagne—a passing cuff for Gramsci, and that's it. Not a look-in for Locke, Hume, Mill, Pareto, Oakeshott—or even Hobbes, whom one might have thought to be in Kissinger's line. Kissinger dilates upon his own 'penchant' for philosophy. Yet only one philosopher, Kant, is mentioned, just once, for an idea from a peripheral essay. In general, it would be hard to imagine a book less touched by Kantian ideas, or by philosophical thought of any sort except the kind executives mean when they talk of 'corporate philosophy'.

Lacking any intellectual distinction, Kissinger's pages—'airless' they are indeed—are leavened only by Washington wisecracks, and large helpings of the pornography of power. We learn much, for instance, about the foibles of Richard Nixon, and this will recommend *The White House Years* to a certain groupie-readership. But what the book lacks above all is any clear sense of the flow and structure of time. Such huge and many-faceted books often append a chronology: here, there is none, nor any firm textual continuum to eliminate the need. William Shawcross has observed that the story of Cambodia—against which, with whatever motive, the White House was directing a vast aerial offensive—is treated for a period in obsessive detail, and then vanishes for years on end from the book's perspective.

Events in *The White House Years* are loosened from their natural conjunctions, and reset elaborately. The story of the Presidency begins with a substantial, indeed over-stuffed account of the European tour of February 1969, in which Nixon appears as peacemaker and conciliator: conducting grand *tours d'horizon* with de Gaulle, dining cosily with Harold Wilson at Chequers, and basking in the repute attaching to the man who was supposedly winding-down America's Asian war (the first business, in any narrative sense, to confront his Presidency). It is 180 pages and many contexts later before the reader learns that the itinerant peacemaker was issuing from his aircraft secret orders (only countermanded at the last moment, and then not for long) to begin the secret bombing of Cambodia.

Again: at page 739 Kissinger has reached July 1971. He is in Pakistan en route to China, enjoying a great 'cops-and-robbers' conspiracy with President Yahya Khan over keeping the Peking diversion secret. Kissinger estimates that this was the last bit of fun 'bluff' Yahya had before being overthrown in consequence of the 'upheaval' in East Pakistan. You have to trudge on to page 853 to reach the rather *earlier* date of April 1971, and Kissinger's acknowledgement that the 'upheaval' consisted largely of acts of genocide committed by the military units under his bluff playmate's command.

Why should the intellectual poverty and narrative curiosities of Kissinger's memoirs matter? First, because his rise to power derived from his status (Harvard certificate) as an intellectual. Nixon, in a phrase Kissinger has used elsewhere, had a 'meatball mind'. He needed to make at least one appointment which would add mental lustre to his administration. He lacked the wide choice that Democratic presidents often enjoy, and he acquired Henry Kissinger (to considerable applause) from Nelson Rockefeller. It is, of course, more usual for people to reach high office by leading trade-unions, running businesses, displaying sitzfleisch-endurance, or just being good with a gun. But Kissinger's qualification is still a very old one, tracing back to the Greeks, to whom it seemed undeniable that intellect—the possession of a mind with unusual capacities for learning and rational introspection—was something which fitted a citizen to rule. In all its sordid adventures, the Western mind has never quite lost track of this idea, and no doubt it is potent in other cultures also.

Lacking any other substantial qualification, Kissinger presents as an unusually pure example of the intellectual drafted into politics: he must therefore be examined as such, just as we would want to know, when examining a soldier's political record, whether his medals were authentic, or obtained from a theatrical costumier's.

What is the essential nature of mind, or intellect—which was, by reputation, Kissinger's title to office, and evidence of which I allege to be lacking from his discourse? Coleridge, in a famous essay, asked himself what distinguished the 'man of superior mind', and decided that it was not, intrinsically, the weight and novelty of his remarks, nor yet their elegance of expression. He thought that it lay centrally in method and arrangement. With an 'ignorant man, though perhaps shrewd and able in his particular calling', we perceive

> ... that the objects and events recur, in the narration in the same order, and with the same accompaniments, however accidental or impertinent, as they had first occured to the narrator...

and Coleridge cites, as a prototype, Mistress Quickly (*Henry IV, Pt 2*):

> ... Thous didst swear to me upon a parcel-gilt goblet, sitting in my Dolphon chamber, at the round table, by a sea-coal fire, on Wednesday in Whitsun week when the prince broke thy head for liking his father to a singing-man of Windsor...

This, at least, is not Kissinger's error—though the one-damn-thing-after-another quality will be recognisable to anyone who has dealt with the memoirs of Harold Wilson—or, still more, the scatological jumble of Nixon's White House tapes. Its cause, in Coleridge's diagnosis, is 'the want of a *staple,* or *starting-post* in the narrator himself: from the absence of the *leading Thought,* which... we may not-inaptly call the INITIATIVE'.

There are more technical and intricate arguments for the notion that the mind must possess an initiative, must set out to invent any world it wishes to perceive—and cannot be a mere receptacle, or 'bucket' in Popper's dismissive phrase. Still, Coleridge's literary models are perhaps more easily assimilable. Given a 'staple' in the narrator, products of intellect are recognisable enough, and

> the first merit, that which admits neither substitute nor equivalent, is, that *everything is in its place.* Where this charm is wanting, every other merit... becomes an additional ground of accusation and regret.

Intellect, like clockwork, will 'divide and announce the silent and otherwise indistinguishable lapse of time', but

> the man of methodical industry and honourable pursuits does more: he realises its ideal divisions, and gives character and individuality to its moments. If the idle are described as killing time, he may justly be said to call it into life and moral being... (making it) the distinct object not only of the consciousness but of the conscience... (rather than that) he lives in time, time lives in him. His days, months and years... will survive the wreck of worlds, and remain extant when time shall be no more.

One asks: does Kissinger's way of dealing with Yahya Khan cause time to become the distinct object of consciousness and conscience?

Coleridge contrasts Mistress Quickly's gabble with some of Shakespeare's tautest verse, in which Hamlet, abord ship, discovers the papers in the death-plot against him ('Up from my cabin/My seagown scarf'd about me, in the dark/Grop'd I find them out; had my desire,/Fingered their packet; and in fine, withdrew/To mine own room again...'). But this kind of writing, in which things 'most remote and diverse in time, place and outward circumstance, are brought into mental contiguity' depends on a balance, and

> when the prerogative of the mind is stretched into despotism, the discourse may degenerate into the grotesque or the fantastical.

In *White House Years,* is everything 'in its place', or does prerogative become despotism? The invasion of Cambodia makes a good case-study, because it is one where extra light is cast on Kissinger's processes by the existence of variorum texts—the published book, that is, and the 'leaked' proofs which show what Kissinger had composed before he saw Shawcross's *Sideshow.*

Kissinger suggests (p.485) that the invasion, in spring 1970, was provoked by Communist onslaughts against Lon Nol: these being supported by the recently-deposed Sihanouk in precipitate alliance with Peking, 'still considered the most revolutionary capital in the world... with which we had no means of communication whatever'. This stuff was inserted post-*Sideshow,* countering Shawcross's allegation that there was little rational motivation involved: seemingly, the job was rushed, because it jars with the passages at p.684-93, where Washington's own precisely-contemporary negotiations with the Peking untouchables are discussed in no small detail. Still, if this is despotism, it is of a kind detectable by the enduring reader.

The invasion was aimed at North Vietnam's 'sanctuaries' inside Cambodia, which had been under secret air attack since the previous year. Naturally, a *provoked* invasion can hardly be pre-meditated, and Kissinger (p.487) says as much:

> There had been no consideration of attacking the sanctuaries before April 21. The final decision was taken on April 28.

Again, a post-*Sideshow* insertion, but accompanied this time with consequential surgery. As first written, this chapter included a memo written for Nixon's use at a meeting on April 26, which said in part:

> The combined US-ARVN operation into Base Area 352-353 (*the Fish Hook area of Cambodia*) has been under preparation by MACV* for several weeks, but up until now secretary Laird has not been aware of the likelihood of its being approved and opposition can be expected from him as well as from the Secretary of State...

Such a document would surely be 'in its place' as part of a chapter on the timing of the invasion decision: most readers would imagine 'several weeks' as going back rather before April 21 from April 26, and would be intrigued by the lack of knowledge attributed to the Secretaries of State (Rogers) and Defence (Laird). But it has vanished from *The White House Years.*

I took up this question of the role of the two Secretaries at Dr Kissinger's London press conference (November, 1979). The published book, I said, recorded the following situation on April 24:

> Since the National Security Council meeting two days earlier, the Secretaries of State and Defence had not been heard from. They knew of contingency plans involving US forces...

---

*Military Assistance Command, Vietnam.

The suggestion conveyed is of men largely complaisant, not ones being actively circumvented. Yet this insertion replaced a quite different passage:

> All planning so far had been conducted without the participation of the Secretaries of State and Defence, who in fact devoted much of their energy to cutting-back on even the South Vietnamese operation into the Parrot's Beak. (*Ed: a much less significant operation, agreed to at the NSC.*)

This suggests that the Secretaries (one of whom, Rogers, was eventually replaced by Kissinger) were not being listened to, rather than not being heard from. It seemed to me, I said to Kissinger, that the new version was aimed at widespread criticism, evoked by *Sideshow,* of White House autocracy. Which one was true?

Both, he replied.

Richard Willson

His lengthy explanation centred on the idea that the two Cabinet officers were only cut out of the system for two days: everything being disclosed to them at an April 26 meeting. This would be a reasonable argument in the context of decision-making stretched over several weeks: but in order to deny premeditation, Kissinger has already destroyed the evidence that anything so long-drawn-out occurred. Most people would feel that two days is quite a time, coming in the latter part of a week when a whole new war is being slapped together.

The sections of the book which confront the events described in *Sideshow* are between pages 239-254 and 457-475, and this is also the extent to which 'variorum' text exists. Most of these pages have significant changes, by insertion or excision or both, and there are several new passages running to hundreds of words. What are we to make of other parts of the book, where the Kissinger version has not been undermined by detailed research, and the effects of the Freedom of Information Act?

Dr Kissinger claims that the changes are such as might be found in the proofs of anyone's memoirs: some indeed are, but not the sort described above. (And it's worth remembering that, before the evidence came out, David Frost taxed him with the suggestion that he had rewritten in an attempt to rebut Shawcross. 'I added to the book exactly one paragraph', said Kissinger, 'and one or two footnotes.') Although he claims to have written a historian's book, the truth appears to be that the past, to Kissinger, is rather like a pack of cards, which can be shuffled and re-shuffled at will. Time, far from being 'called into moral being', is thus assassinated: it contains no trajectory which might confront the hero of *the White House Years* with a real human dilemma, such as the handling of personal relationships when trying (notionally, anyway) to use a beastly regime like Yahya's for some higher purpose. Vast mental agility is required to juggle such masses of material, and surely no other living politician could attempt it. But this is not intellect at work, it is anti-intellect: the book is a kind of Black Hole of consciousness.

What really happened in Indochina? Essentially, the American enterprise was always impossible. This is not an equation which can be much affected by making out the best possible case for the South Vietnamese regime and the worst possible case for the communists: the essential term consisted in the fact that the communists were always in possession of Vietnam's ancient, inflexible nationalism. The nation involved has more than 50 million people. Therefore the communists could only be defeated by large land forces, taking heavy casualties. These were unavailable—not through epidemic American cowardice, but for lack of a Vietnamese attack on Pearl Harbour.

Aerial bombardment and high-technology warfare were a delusion. Deployed by a superpower, they may wreck societies, but they cannot hold military or political territory. Therefore, the concrete choice the West had to make in Indochina was not between liberal democracy and international communism. It was a choice about the level of destruction to be applied to nationalist communism in the course of its predictable, local victory: the level eventually imposed (though short of nuclear holocaust) was horribly disproportionate to the merits of the dispute.

In this situation, those who resist a movement may indeed be responsible for the form it assumes. The thought is moderately complicated within a context dominated by the 1939-45 model of war as a conflict between peoples of roughly equivalent development. The issue is therefore readily oversimplified by exercise of mental agility. 'We destabilised Cambodia', said Kissinger at the press conference, 'the way Britain destabilised Poland in 1939.' This could only deceive people (but they are a majority) whose knowledge about Indochina is vestigial: discourse becomes grotesque and fantastical when mind is employed to manufacture such comparisons.

Nobody accurately foresaw the Khmer Rouge nightmare, or contends that Kissinger should have. But what is clear is that when Kissinger and Nixon began their work, the Khmer Rouge was a splinter group, no more capable of achieving power than the Bolsheviks could have prevailed without the carnage and chaos of the first world war. And the disaster precipitated by America's aerial bombardment and invasion was no lesser in its impact on that small and vulnerable society. To be sure, one cannot predict just what will happen to a society if one props up a corrupt puppet like Lon Nol as its ruler, for five years, saturating its countryside with high explosive in an effort to preserve him. But one can predict that it will be nothing good, and it is mere sleight-of-hand to suggest that such actions can be retrospectively sanctified by the emergence of Pol Pot.

Tirelessly shuffling his pack, Kissinger suggests that the North Vietnamese caused everything by using Cambodian territory for their bases and supply-routes, thus violating neutrality before he and Nixon did. True, the law sometimes allows one offence to cancel out another, but only if restraint and proportionality are applied—as any landowner will find if he pleads justifiable homicide after machine-gunning a few trespassers on a tenant's farm. The practical truth is that America's 'defence' of Cambodia's shaky neutrality never looked like doing anything but blow every vestige of it apart. All the real evidence suggests that the widening of the war into Cambodia was an irrational act: Kissinger's whole book is an attempt, by means of misdirection, elision, suppression and narrative disaggregation to clothe this and other irrationalities in the appearance of sober statesmanship. He receives the accolade for this from Dr David Owen in *The Times* ('on... the delicate balance of power which determines our survival, he is... careful, clear-headed, constrained and consistent.')

The real story, to which *The White House Years* relates chiefly as a huge, oppressive mirage, is of an attempted application of the Madman Theory of War—more academically, an attempt to cash in the significant premium attaching to irrationality. Nixon, boozing in front of the image of *Patton*, was no doubt taken with this idea, but its elaboration was surely beyond him. A pretence of intellectualism would have been required for that. Also, of course, a carapace of secrecy, for in the nuclear age any democratic politician who confesses to the practice of irrationality will be smartly booted out. (The non-democratic solution is probably a bullet.) More publicly, Kissinger and Nixon deployed the accompanying idea of 'linkage': a misapplication to international affairs of the simplistic causality in the old rhyme about the fire that made the stick beat the dog, which made the dog bite the pig, and in turn made the pig jump over the stile.

On this scheme, which Kissinger claims to have adumbrated at the outset, the idea was that the USSR, in order to obtain Middle East peace settlements, trade concession, SALT agreements and other goodies, would be persuaded to persuade the North Vietnamese to give up the aims for which they had fought without compromise for 20 years. This was not a very good idea: a better one would have been to use Nixon's conservative credentials, then unassailable, to persuade the American public that a war in which casualties are not acceptable must be abandoned.

However, it was in outline something to which rational thought could be applied. And indeed the Russians (who certainly had influence though not control in Hanoi) tried to respond. The Soviet ambassador to Washington, Anatoly Dobrynin, asked Kissinger in May 1969: 'Supposing the war were settled, how would you go about improving relations?' To this Kissinger says (p.161) he could not 'answer in precise terms'. This is pretty amazing, seeing that we learn on p.226 that the Indochina war was by that time so serious a problem in America that 'the comity by which a democratic society must live had broken down'.

The truth about the secret bombing of communist base areas inside Cambodia (which had already begun by then) and the invasion which occurred a year later is not that they were provoked in any genuine sense by the communist offensives which were going on. They were stratagems, designed as best they could to evade the democratic restrictions of the US constitution, to convince Hanoi of Nixon's endless bellicosity, and to implant the fear that worse could yet befall. With terror thus injected into the apparatus of 'linkage' a famous victory was to be procurred. It was a scheme of horrible recklessness, and Watergate was born out of the distortions it produced.

But the real price for this recklessness was paid, and continues to be paid, by the Cambodians. It may be worth saying, that only a pseudo-intellectual could embrace the profoundly absurd idea that irrationality can ever have calculable consequences.

Nobody needs telling that the defence of democracy is perilous. But many people still believe that 'geopolitics' can offer help, and Kissinger's ponderous memoirs are designed to reinforce that belief. They are not designed to be read, so much as to convey awe through their vast bulk and meaningless detail. The majority of people are honest, busy and aware that intellectual effort is difficult. It is an easy step to assume that any difficult book is a work of intellect.

Like many nonsense-systems, 'geopolitics' begins with the reasonable observation that nations bargain somewhat like individuals. You don't sell your car at a friendly price to someone who steals your mother's lettuces. But the 'somewhat' doesn't go very far, and Kissinger's account, once stripped of persiflage, is perceptibly absurd. It is: 'How we dragged our heels on SALT and the Middle East and East-West trade, while we frightened the Vietnamese (oh, yes, and the *bad* Cambodians—same thing) and drove the Russians out of their minds (as Nixon put it) by cuddling up to the Chinese (bit of a shock to the Japanese), which involved 'tilting' towards Pakistan, as against India, 'cos the Pakistanis were putting us in touch with the Chinese (tough darts, Sheikh Mujib, but writing a letter would have been too simple), in order to make the Russians do a better deal on SALT, or West Berlin, or anyway stop bugging us.' It's perhaps understandable that even the Grand Master could not give a precise answer when Dobrynin asked him what was going on.

Geopolitics, in fact, has the same relationship as chess to real warfare and real politics—which is to say, no significant relationship whatever. The qualification for expounding it is an inability to tell the difference between men and chessmen.

The rules of chess are certainly complex enough to generate an enormous array of situation. But the 'rules' of the real world, insofar as we know them at all, are infinitely more complex, and uncertain. Because of this, moral intuition is just as necessary as rationalising power in the attempt to chart a passage; indeed, 'mind', or 'intelligence', which the Greeks taught us to respect, consists in their intimate, active fusion. Kissinger's book is an exercise in separating them.

(23 November 1979)

Interview with Le Duc Tho

Anthony Barnett

Is Henry Kissinger's book *The White House Years* a reliable record of US activity during the Nixon administration? One person in a position to answer this question is Le Duc Tho, the Hanoi Politbureau member who sat opposite Kissinger for many hours in the negotiating sessions which led to the Paris Peace Accords. A substantial part of Kissinger's book is concerned with these talks. Le Duc Tho challenges Kissinger's veracity, and is scornful of his world view. He sees him as a man outdated by at least a century.

I sought out Le Duc Tho's views on a recent trip to the Vietnamese capital. I put down questions in writing, and asked for a written response in English. This seemed both the most exact procedure, given the length of Kissinger's book, and the one most likely to succeed.

The administration in Hanoi is extremely baffling. It combines extremes of competence and inefficiency, people are both unnecessarily secretive and unexpectedly frank. Relations with Westerners are contradictory, in a way which perhaps reflects recent history. The anti-war movement assisted the Vietnamese and they are grateful, yet at the same time their country has been singled out for military and political victimisation.

Le Duc Tho's response to my questions was only delivered on the penultimate day of my stay. I was therefore unable to put supplementary questions to him. Nonetheless, I had taken the opportunity to register certain differences between interviewer and interviewee. When it seemed possible that my suggestion would be accepted I put down three types of questions: those concerned with Kissinger's book, some about the actual negotiations so far as Cambodia was concerned, and others on more general matters. These latter ranged from relations to China and the USSR, to Vietnam's historic expansion southwards and its attempt to conquer Cambodia in the 1830s (which was a costly failure). I made it clear that my analysis of China differed from Hanoi's official view, and I suggested that it was time to abandon Ho Chi Minh's tradition of not speaking openly about differences with fraternal countries, an aspect of political democracy particularly important for Cambodia. Le Duc Tho decided that he could answer for the record only the first two sets of questions. In a private talk he alluded to some of the others, and I also discussed these with Vietnam's new Foreign Minister Nguyen Co Thach.

The obvious come-back question which follows from Le Duc Tho's replies concerns Cambodia. He emphasises that Hanoi assisted the Khmer revolutionaries, yet denounces their leader as 'more Maoist than Mao'. Why then did Vietnam back Pol Pot through 1976? It seems that Hanoi viewed his animosity towards the Vietnamese as an understandable expression of nationalism, which would at least guarantee Cambodia's independence from Peking.

If this was so, it was a fatal miscalculation. Today, the Vietnamese do not fully believe what happened in Cambodia, despite their propaganda about the 'genocidal Pol Pot Ieng Sary clique'. Le Duc Tho could laugh at Kissinger. He was composed when he discussed policy in Cambodia today; Vietnamese forces would not get bogged down, and would in time withdraw, he insisted.

But when he spoke of Pol Pot a genuine pre-occupation seemed to emerge. The Cambodian people do not understand how it could have happened, nor do the Vietnamese, he stated, and he went on to urge foreign scholars to help explain how Pol Pot's regime could have come about. A note of inquiry about the modern world was struck that cannot be found at all in Kissinger's memoirs. Perhaps it was due to this capacity that, in the end, Le Duc Tho got the better of the American.

Question: In an interview you gave to Cora Weiss at the end of 1973, you said: 'During our talks I told Kissinger that I will not write a book. He said he would. I said: "Do not distort the truth".'

Are there any distortions or omissions in his account of the negotiations?

Answer: The *New Statesman* review called the memoirs of Kissinger 'a web of untruths'. In my opinion, this is a quite precise assessment.

As everybody knows, the United States could have come out of Vietnam in 1969. But the Nixon-Kissinger administration nurtured an illusion of using 'Vietnamisation' of the war together with the 'China card' to pull out of South Vietnam militarily—while still maintaining its presence politically through the puppet administration in Saigon. Its aim was to perpetuate the partition of Vietnam.

But the United States had to pull out militarily, which led to the collapse of the Thieu administration and the complete liberation of South Vietnam. That was the biggest ever setback for the United States. Mr Kissinger cannot tell the truth about this.

Instead, Mr Kissinger has tried to 'rewrite history' in an attempt to claim as his own success the policy which led to the setback. He attempts to justify the crimes that the Nixon-Kissinger administration further perpetrated against the Indochinese peoples and the additional losses in lives, money, material and national dignity to the United States which they caused. That is the main distortion in the chapters dealing with the war in Vietnam and Indochina.

The book says that the United States had to carry out B52 bombing at the end of 1972, because Vietnam wanted to prolong the negotiations and refused to sign the agreement the fundamental content of which had been agreed upon by both sides in October.

As a matter of fact, it was the United States that did a complete about-face. As both sides had agreed, Kissinger should have come to Hanoi on 23 October 1972 to initial the Agreement, which could have been officially signed on 31 October 1972. On 21 October 1972, Nixon sent a message to Prime Minister Pham Van Dong saying that the United States 'considers the Agreement complete'.

But on the *following* day, 22 October, Kissinger said it was still necessary to hold another session and, therefore, the Agreement could not be signed on 31 October.

That was why the negotiation was prolonged, solely because of the United States.

The US manoeuvre in that terror bombing was that the Nixon-Kissinger administration hoped it could seriously weaken the potentialities of the Democratic Republic of Vietnam, thereby forcing us to accept additional terms posed by the United States. On the contrary, the US lost 32 B52s, together with many pilots captured or killed. At the same time there was angry condemnation of the Nixon and Kissinger administration by world opinion, including opinion in the US itself. The victory of this 'Dien Bien Phu in the air' compelled the United States to sign an Agreement the content of which was not in the main different from that in October.

The book claims that I had 'secretly' told Kissinger that 'the mission of the Vietnamese people was not only to take over South Vietnam but to dominate the whole of Indochina as well'. This is a brazen fabrication.

In fact, when Mr Kissinger asked me to discuss the 'neutralisation' of Kampuchea (Cambodia), I told him that he and I had only the right to discuss the Vietnam problem.

To understand why he has made up such 'secret' remarks, you must remember that the book also serves Kissinger's desire to return to office—despite his record of war crimes. So he had joined in a new anti-Vietnam campaign, in which Washington and Peking are now engaged.

The book also states that I had suggested to Mr Kissinger that Thieu should be eliminated. This too is a fabrication. We did not fight against one person, but against the entire reactionary regime. The elimination of the individual chieftain is the traditional job of the United States.

It was the United States that had previously eliminated Diem, and Mr Kissinger himself suggested more than once that Thieu should be replaced by big Minh*.

I told him once that 'you are a liar'. Even his close associates, Helmut Sonnefeldt, for example, also confirmed that he 'tells lies because that is his nature'.

Question: What is your estimate of Kissinger's real role in US policy making? In the aftermath of Nixon's downfall some people are presenting Kissinger as the main architect of American foreign policy, especially with regard to China. Kissinger himself, however, in the midst of one policy crisis, over India, said: 'We are the President's men'. Although a skilful servant of power, was Kissinger ever in fact its master?

Answer: When successful, Mr Kissinger wants to claim his own contribution. When failing to achieve success, he shifts the responsibility on to Nixon.

Notwithstanding, Nixon and Kissinger complement each other to such an extent that public opinion calls them 'Nissinger'. And both of them must be held responsible for the US foreign policy in the years 1968-74.

Kissinger typified post Second World War US diplomacy—its aggressive nature and arrogance. That is why, although politically he sometimes praised highly the policy of negotiation and compromise, basically, he attempted to use military strength. Threats, treachery and deception were his stock in trade.

Yet he is living in the 20th century. The balance of forces favours socialism, national independence, peace and democracy. Kissinger is under the illusion that he can repeat the 19th century policy of Metternich, and in his vanity he thinks this shows his mastery of realpolitik.

---

* A tall general who became president in the last hours of the Saigon regime.

Actually, he and Nixon were naive and their compatriots who opposed the war were more realistic. Today his effort to justify the past could lead to further setbacks. The same applies to China, as it has already discovered through its support of Pol Pot aggression against Vietnam.

Question: Kissinger presents the Paris Peace Accords as a complete triumph for Nixon's and his diplomacy. He presents an interpretation of the Accords in which they are seen as allowing the US to provide unlimited military supplies to the Thieu regime, as prohibiting the replacement of North Vietnamese forces south of the old DMZ, and as preserving the Saigon Government. He states that Nixon would have used 'the means necessary to enforce a peace'. Recently, an American liberal columnist, Anthony Lewis, described the Christmas bombing as establishing a level of violence that America would be prepared to repeat, to maintain peace (*New York Times*, 2/12/79). Do you think this is accurate? If so, to what extent did you realise at the time that Nixon considered the withdrawal of US troops as a means of perpetuating the bombing?

Answer: The objectives of the Nixon-Kissinger administration in the Paris Agreement were to withdraw the US troops but at the same time to maintain the puppet administration to implement its neo-colonialism in South Vietnam.
The United States, in fact, was compelled:
● To recognise all the fundamental national rights of the Vietnamese people written down in Chapter 1, Article 1 of the Agreement.
● To accept the presence of Vietnamese armed forces in South Vietnam while the United States had to withdraw all its troops from South Vietnam.
● To accept the existence of two zones of control, two administrations, two armies and three political forces in South Vietnam.
These provisions created extremely favourable conditions, both military and political, for the victorious Spring 1975 general offensives completely to liberate the South and reunify our Motherland.

Question: Kissinger treats Watergate and the downfall of the Nixon presidency as an arbitrary and irrational event, quite unconnected to the way Nixon conducted policy. Yet the secret telephone tapping and other manoeuvres against political opponents began with the 'secret' bombing of Cambodia and Nixon's decision to obtain a military victory despite US opinion. How did you view Watergate? Did your interpretation of it change at all, as it developed?

Answer: The Watergate scandal was the biggest and worst political crisis in the US history and also a natural aftermath of the aggressive war in Indochina, and dirty tricks carried out by successive US administrations, particularly the Nixon administration in an attempt to conceal their deeds from and deceive the American people.

Question: In your Foreign Ministry's White Paper, '*The Truth about Vietnam-Chinese relations over the last thirty years*', Mao's inviting Nixon to Peking is described as a decisive turning point and a betrayal of the Vietnamese, the Indochinese, and the world revolutions. What do you think would have happened if Mao had not imposed this policy?

Answer: If the Peking ruling circles had pursued a correct revolutionary line, the fight of the Vietnamese people would have had much better conditions on the way to victory and US imperialism would have met even more difficulties and the world revolutionary movement would certainly have been marked by more vigorous developments. Nonetheless, the revolutionary currents will continue to develop.

Question: In the White Paper, America and China are charged with making a deal in which the delivery of a divided Vietnam and a stable Thieu regime would be traded for Peking's supremacy over Taiwan. Indeed Kissinger states specifically that there was a 'linkage' between Taiwan and Vietnam established in the Shanghai communiqué (*The White House Years*, p.1077). He also says that around the issue of Taiwan there was not 'a sharp bargain but... a joint understanding'. What, in your opinion, was the understanding reached by the US and China in 1972?

Answer: The 1972 Agreement between the United States and China marked the beginning of the open and comprehensive collusion between imperialism and the Peking rulers. It meant that the US would be assisted by China to settle the Vietnam question to the advantage of the US and disadvantage of Vietnam, and would use the 'China card' to oppose the Soviet Union and the world revolutionary movement.

Exploiting the United States' need to solve the Vietnam question in its favour, and its anti-Soviet and anti-world-revolution positions, the Chinese rulers attempted to turn China into one of the three world superpowers, so as to have a say in solving international problems, especially in Asia, and to seek a solution for the Taiwan question.

Question: When the US demanded changes and commitments in addition to your draft of the Accords, did it try to pressure Vietnam into a Cambodian cease-fire? In particular, it has been said, by Cambodians, that the Christmas bombing was in part an attempt to get a Cambodian settlement, and that Kissinger threatened Hanoi, should Phnom Penh fall to the Khmer Rouge. Is this true?

Answer: Our position was that Vietnam should not negotiate on Kampuchea's behalf. Vietnam respected the independence and sovereignty of the Kampuchean people and supported them, whether negotiating or fighting.

The aims of the Christmas B52 bombing by the US were not to put pressure on Vietnam so as to obtain a solution to Kampuchea, I have discussed its purpose above.

Kissinger made no threat as to the possibility of Phnom Penh falling to Pol Pot-Ieng Sary, and we ourselves helped the Kampuchean people and contributed to the liberation of Phnom Penh.

Question: What did Kissinger say the United States would do to Cambodia, if a cease-fire was not obtained there?

Answer: Mr Kissinger made no reference to this question.

Question: It has been argued, I think plausibly, that the tremendously intensive American bombing of Cambodia from January to August 1973, so brutalised the countryside and punished the revolutionary forces, that it helped to create the social and psychological conditions that made the draconian measures of the Pol Pot regime possible. But if Pol Pot had accepted a cease-fire the bombing would not have taken place. Furthermore, the revolutionary forces were perhaps better placed to go over to political struggle in Cambodia than they were in South Vietnam. Why did Pol Pot refuse a cease-fire in 1973, in your view? What arguments were put to the Cambodian leadership by Pham Hung, when talks were held in Cambodia at that time? What do you think would have happened had they agreed to a cease-fire?

Answer: The bombing of Kampuchea from January to August 1973 was not much heavier than before. If comparison is to be made according to the American sources, the amount of US bombs dropped in Laos and North Vietnam was much more than that dropped in Kampuchea.

The genocidal policy of Pol Pot-Ieng Sary was in the main more Maoist than Mao's, was abetted and aided by the Peking rulers and had nothing to do with the US bombing in Kampuchea. Shortly before Phnom Penh was liberated, they had already started a cruel and much-hated policy in newly liberated areas.

In their mind, a cease-fire at that time was not to their advantage. With the Paris Agreement signed, they knew that the US defeat was obvious. The Agreement paved the way and created favourable conditions, both military and political, for the victory of the Kampuchean revolution. Therefore, they wanted to fight to the end in order to seize total power in Kampuchea, rather than to have a cease-fire and then to negotiate a political solution.

Question: Given the importance of these issues. did you try to circulate your own arguments and explain your own policy to Cambodian cadres, given that your forces were there at the time?

Answer: It is our view-point that the affairs of Kampuchea are to be settled by the Kampucheans.

Question: How did you relate to the Cambodian revolution after the breach of 1973? Did you make any efforts to supply aid and assistance? Were Vietnamese forces able to obtain rice supplies from Cambodia at all?

Answer: After 1973, the Vietnamese forces were faced with obstacles created by Pol Pot, to their moving about and purchasing necessary foodstuffs. Yet we continued giving them aid and helped them in the transportation of weapons and ammunitions and assisted them in other necessary things in the liberation of Phnom Penh.

(21 March 1980)

Part III
Cambodia

Letting a nation die
John Pilger

I have just returned from Cambodia. During 20 years as a journalist, most of them
spent in transit at wars and places of contrived upheaval, I had not seen anything
to compare with what I saw in Cambodia. Nor did my expectation, based upon the
stories of refugees and rumour, in any way match the reality; for what has
happened there has not happened before.

Among the five of us who went—the others were an ATV television team and
photographer Eric Piper—two concerns quickly developed. Was it possible, we
asked ourselves, to encapsulate the evidence of what we saw, and what seemed
barely credible, in a way that the *enormity* of the crime and its aftermath might be
recognised internationally and the survivors, who are mostly sick and starving
children, might be saved. The second concern was almost surreal: how to keep
moving *away* from the rush of sounds and images that pursued us every day; and of
course that was not possible; the screams of fleshless, dying children remain
indelible.

In the 'hospital' of an orphanage in Phnom Penh, laid out like a Great War field
station in the Gothic shell of an abandoned chapel, there were children who had
been found wandering in the forest, living off treebark, grass and poisonous
plants. Their appearance almost denied their humanity: rows of staring, manic
eyes set in skin like the frayed cloth of a tailor's dummy; once our filming had to
stop while Gerry Pinches, the cameraman, walked away to cry. In the city's
'peoples hospital', where every piece of modern equipment had been mutilated by
the Khmer Rouge and the dispensary was bare, the cries of children reached such a
crescendo that they could be heard in the street outside. When we returned the
next morning, another six had wasted to death: their names chalked on a black-
board beside a poster reminding us that 1979 was the International Year of the
Child. There were no antibiotics, no antiseptics, no anaesthetic, no anti-malarials,
no vitamins, no painkillers: not even an aspirin. Food was a gruel of 'dirty' rice and
it came in a small condensed milk tin; there was no milk.

On the roof of this hospital is a large red cross, a remnant of the days when
ladders of bombs fell from B-52s a few miles away. The red cross is, of course, a
universal symbol of humanitarianism, which is said to transcend politics and
frontiers. At this hospital it might as well ward off evil spirits. No International

CAMBODIA
Major towns and refugee camps

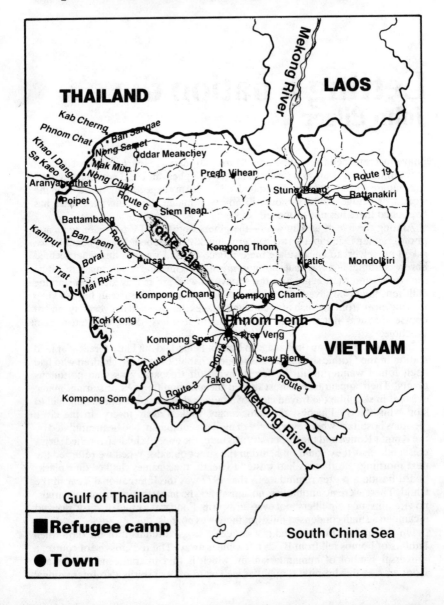

Red Cross doctors or nurses have come; driblets of Red Cross medicines have come and have evaporated. When Jacques Beaumont, the representative of UNICEF, the United Nations Children's Fund, stood before our camera to be interviewed, he, too, wept. 'I am from the United Nations', he said, 'but I have only my suitcases'.

The day before, in a village in the south, Beaumont had watched four starving children die... 'and me with only my suitcases', he repeated. In the province of Kompong Speu, at least half the children we filmed in an 'orphans ward', a straw hut, are now dead. 'Anyway, they will all go soon', said Dr Jean-Michael Vinot, one of two French doctors who travelled with us: the *only* Western doctors who had come to help. Most of the children are dying from nutrition related diseases that are preventable and curable. Anthrax, contracted from eating contaminated meat, kills within a month. Penicillin can stop it; astonishingly, there is some penicillin at Kompong Speu, but it is not enough, and each morning the Vietnamese doctor must choose who will live and who will die. More often than not the choice is made for him.

I remember Cambodia from before the bombing and the horror of the Khmer Rouge. Perhaps I romanticise, but it seemed the most inoffensive and graceful land, whose people cherished their obscurity and never held out a begging bowl and never knew hunger. In his excellent book, *Sideshow*, William Shawcross quotes a 1959 Pentagon report describing the Khmer people as 'by and large a passive and docile people' who could not be easily panicked, whose horizons were limited to village, pagoda and forest, who knew of no other countries, who respected their government, who feared ghosts and 'cannot be counted upon to act in any positive way for the benefit of US aims and policies'.

In other words, they were expendable. Eleven years later American foreign policy pivoted on Henry Kissinger's 'Theory of Expendability'. This 'doctrine' (a word that pleased Kissinger) assumed that all the world was a chess game in which the small nations were mere pawns to be moved at will, or to be declared expendable, regardless of questions of sovereignty, morality etc., and that the crushing or isolating or starving of these troublesome lands could be accommodated or negotiated in the spirit of detente between the super powers. (Not surprisingly, it is a view shared with enthusiasm by the Kremlin, which is currently attempting to crush 'expendable' Eritrea, without, of course, a murmur from the West.)

Cambodia was Kissinger's first opportunity to put his theory into practice. Cambodia was neutral, 'by and large passive and docile' and allied to no bloc; Cambodia could be broken in order to demonstrate to the neighbouring Vietnamese communists the 'toughness' of the Nixon administration. This 'theory' became a terrible reality over the skies of Cambodia in March 1970, and the bombing, which had no justification in American law and was against the wishes of Congress, continued for three years. The equivalent, in tons of bombs, of five Hiroshimas was dropped on once peaceful Cambodia: the greatest aerial bombardment ever. 'The Khmer Rouge', as Shawcross makes clear in *Sideshow*, 'were born out of the inferno...' The Khmer Rouge ideologues, such as they were, had modelled their revolution on the political vandalism of Mao's cultural revolution. They had no popular base among the Khmer people, who preferred the traditions of Buddhist harmony to upheaval, and their 'revolution' lacked an external catalyst. The 'inferno' of the Kissinger bombing provided that catalyst.

Today, the process begun by Kissinger is nearing completion. Between a million and a half and three million people died during the four years of Khmer Rouge terror, and the survivors now face the real prospect of their extinction. 'We have six months to save three million people, the majority of the population, from starvation and related diseases', said Jacques Beaumont. 'Six months is the maximum. Eighty-five per cent of the women have stopped menstruating, because they are malnourished and exhausted and, like everybody, they have not recovered from the trauma of the terror. So where is the next generation coming from?'

Cambodia will be the first 'expendable' nation to die, not because it cannot survive the killing of perhaps a third of its population, but because it cannot sustain the complementary effect: the denial of relief. It is interesting that those who have led this land to the edge of death share a particular style. They have taken their decisions to bomb and to refuse humanitarian help at great remove in distance and responsibility from the consequences of their obduracy; not for them the sight of an emaciated child spitting itself to death!

In 1977, Roger Morris, a former member of Kissinger's National Security Council staff, wrote a book called *Uncertain Greatness,* in which he describes how the President's foreign policy advisers, the 'Wise Men', prepared the ground for the destruction of Indochina. 'Though they spoke of terrible human suffering', wrote Morris, 'reality was sealed off by their trite, lifeless vernacular: "capabilities", "objectives", "our chips", "giveaway". It was a matter, too, of culture and style. They spoke with the cool, deliberate detachment of men who believe that the banishment of feeling renders them wise and, more important, credible to other men'. Of Kissinger and Nixon, Morris wrote succinctly: 'They neither understood the foreign policy they were dealing with nor were moved deeply by the bloodshed and suffering they administered to their stereotypes'.

Give or take a few words, the same might be said of those politicians and foreign policy bureaucrats, notably our own, who now allow Cambodia to die. The United States, which sent its most lethal bombers over Cambodia, has not sent *one* relief plane. Europe, urged on by Mrs Thatcher, has cut off all food aid to Vietnam, Cambodia's *only* reliable source of food. The EEC's surplus food 'mountains' will be sold cheaply to the Russians, or they will remain intact. *Six* relief planes have landed at Phnom Penh in the ten months since the Khmer Rouge were routed by the Vietnamese. UNICEF and the International Committee of the Red Cross together have contributed modestly to several plane-loads, which, in terms of effective relief, is virtually nothing. Perhaps never before has there been such a unity of indifference toward a great human tragedy. The Theory of Expendability, it seems, has gained universal acceptance.

Coming back to Phnom Penh is dream-like. Twelve years ago, I flew across from wartime Saigon, exchanging venality and neurosis for doe-eyed charm. On Sundays the parade down Monivong Avenue was a joy: the parasols, the girls with jasmine astride Hondas, the saffron robes, the platoons of well-fed families, the ice cream barrows, the hustlers. You awoke at the Hotel Royale, switched on your radio and, in all probability, heard the squeaky, drama-queen voice of Prince Sihanouk berating a foreign reporter for producing yet another article about the financial excesses of the royal family. This happened to an American friend of mine who, later that day, was summoned to the royal palace and ordered to listen, in dutiful silence, to the Prince's Oscar Peterson collection: such was his 'punishment'. Such was Cambodia: feudal, corrupt, unpredictable, preposterous, prosperous and at peace in a cockpit of unending war.

Today, Phnom Penn is a dead place, except for groups of ragged, hungry people in peasant-black, who forage like crows in the parks, courtyards, offices, cinemas, filling stations. The majority are children and orphans. An eight-year-old confines himself to a wardrobe on its side, in the street; an emaciated infant drifts down the centre of the main thoroughfare, without an echo of its other days. With every monsoonal downpour the gutters are sluiced with money, which pours from the crushed National Bank. The Khmer Rouge, in their mania to eradicate anything and anyone linked to 'the dead age of greed and machines', sought out symbols. The National Library was converted to a pigsty and its volumes burned or thrown into the streets; all books and learning were 'illegal'. The medicine school was painted bright red and its equipment destroyed; modern medicine was 'banned'. A 19th century Gothic cathedral, which stood at the city centre, was *erased;* not a stone remains. Pagodas were pulverised, as if by a demolition squad; all religion, decreed the constitution of Democratic Kampuchea, was 'detrimental and therefore wrong'.

On 17 April 1975, the day the Khmer Rouge entered the capital, car owners were ordered to throw away their ignition keys and push their cars to a dump on the edge of the city. It is a Luddites' shrine, a cemetery of machines: cars, ambulances, fire engines, typewriters, generators, television sets. There is a separate pile of burned telephones; all modern communications, including post, were 'illegal'. Great shade trees, planted by the French, were cut down for no apparent reason. Any structure of brick or stone was condemned as belonging to 'the dead age'. In Kompong Thom province 180 schools were destroyed; *two* remain intact.

Outside Phnom Penh, in 'regroupment centres', people wait patiently to enter the city. Among them, former residents are hard to find; some two and a half million people were ordered out of the city at gunpoint on that April day and most of them are said to be 'missing'. Middle class people, professional people and skilled workers are rare; 48 doctors remain out of 550. At the last census there were 11,000 university students; there are now 450. Out of 106,000 secondary school children, 5,300 have been found. The killing appears to have been most widespread among children of primary school age. Out of 991,000 children, 322,379 survive.

Of course, the numbers of survivors will grow as people lose their fear of 'coming forward', which invariably meant death under the Khmer Rouge. Hark Sarinn, a former teacher who now helps to run an orphanage, went recently into the regroupment camps with a tannoy. 'Who is a teacher? Who is a water engineer?' he asked. 'Don't be frightened... you are needed.' There was silence. In one day three young men, vibrating with fear, revealed for the first time in four and a half years that they were university students. Our camera seemed to help restore confidence. Those who shook their heads when our interpreter asked if they spoke any English or French would wait, then let a few words tumble out; knowledge of a foreign language, they told us, meant executions.

A young woman told me in French how sixteen members of her family had been executed in one day: 'They were declared to be unproductive', she said. 'They were killed with tree branches and their throats were slit... one by one. My baby was left in the heat while I was forced to husk the rice. When I came back he was dead.' She said this, and much more, without emotion, as if her grief and shock were incubated forever. Sorrow was regarded as implied criticism of the 'Angkar'—the unseen 'organisation', whose 'wisdom' guided the 'purified and glorious Khmer society'. In a society such as Cambodia's, the extended family forms the fabric of the nation and, with almost every family now decimated, the nation itself has unravelled. To watch the expressions of relatives searching at a mass grave, near the temples of Angkor Wat, kneeling beside hundreds of skulls and bones, is to watch the mental collapse of a whole section of humanity. And they ask only for food.

In July 1979, most of the senior tier of the US State Department gave evidence before a Senate hearing on Indochina refugees. The Secretary of State, Cyrus Vance, agreed that Cambodia faced 'a very grave famine'. The *Washington Post* reported

> The United States has been frustrated in its efforts to work through international organisations and other governments to head off potential starvation, according to State Department witnesses. The United States is prohibited by law from aiding Cambodia directly...
>
> (The officials said) the International Committee of the Red Cross reportedly was told by the Phnom Penh authorities that no food is needed, but Red Cross officials are in the Cambodian capital now for further discussions.
>
> Dick Clark, the State Department's refugee coordinator told Senator Kennedy that the United States is prepared to work with 'any qualified international group' to head off famine in Cambodia.

There must be few examples of official deception as blatant as the above. *No* American humanitarian aid has reached Cambodia for two reasons: none has been offered and the International Committee of the Red Cross and UNICEF—the two 'qualified international groups', through which the United States and other Western countries' governments usually send aid to regimes they do not recognise—have made no move to mount a substantial relief programme. The Phnom Penh Government appealed for relief at the beginning of July and a written request for 100,000 tons of rice, 15,000 tons of sugar and 8,000 tons of butter oil, as well as medical supplies, was handed to three ICRC officials. Two months have since passed, countless thousands have died needlessly.

A senior British relief agency official told me last week, 'The ICRC and UNICEF are fully aware of how urgent the situation is. They have worked out a joint plan to send 700 tons of relief a week and, with luck, this may begin on 29 September. Both have been blocked by politics. The Pol Pot regime is still recognised by the General Assembly and UNICEF has become ensnarled in the anti-Vietnam campaign. The ICRC may protest its neutrality, but it has become susceptible to pressure, mostly from Washington, not to rush into Cambodia as this may well lead to de facto recognition of the Heng Samrin government and blow away the notion of Vietnam as "aggressor" and the main obstacle to getting relief in. The ICRC also wants a foothold in China, and China is Pol Pot's most powerful ally. It is a nasty, messy business.'

The ICRC's denial of aid to Cambodia was borne out by a rather melodramatic meeting I had with one of its representatives in Phnom Penh. During my interview with Jacques Beaumont, I asked him why UNICEF had done so little. At this, he marched away from the camera and led the director, David Munro, and me to a distraught Red Cross man. '*He* will explain', said Beaumont. The Red Cross man asked me if I, being Australian, had contacts in the Australian Government who might arrange the despatch of a Hercules C-130 cargo plane. 'With transport, food and drugs', he said, 'one of these planes would save thousands of lives *now*.' I asked why the ICRC itself did not approach the Australian Government. 'I am desperate,' he said, 'People are dying around us. They can't wait for the politics to be ironed out.'

Another lethal myth, propagated by the State Department and by the Foreign Office, is that the Vietnamese are preventing aid reaching Cambodia. Jim Howard, a veteran Oxfam official who recently returned from Cambodia, told me, 'The Vietnamese gave me total co-operation. They offered transport, even pilots. I am going to Bangkok this week to hire a ship. The real obstacle is getting governments to join us. Those people out there *can* be saved, but only governments can do it. One tanker with 100,000 tons of rice would feed everybody for two months.'

Perversely, Cambodia is a relief agency's dream come true. There are few bureaucrats to 'interfere', because few have been found alive. The Ministry of Health consists of a Minister, his deputy, an interpreter and an old Renault. The DC-8 charter that brought Jim Howard flew directly to Phnom Penh and landed, unannounced, at 11 in the morning. By four o'clock that afternoon its cargo of antibiotics and milk was being given to the children.

In Phnom Penh I asked the Vietnamese Ambassador, Vo Doan Giang, what his and the Cambodian government's attitude was to relief from the West. He replied, '*Any* relief can come without *any* conditions.' 'Are you sure?' I asked. 'No conditions', he repeated. 'Do we want this country to die?' I pressed this point again in Hanoi with Vietnam's Foreign Minister, Nguyen Co Thach. 'We welcome *all* humanitarian aid', he said. 'At present we have to share one grain of salt between two poor peoples. We don't have two grains of salt, and we ourselves have a famine coming! The burden of sick Cambodia and Vietnam is enormous and senior Vietnamese officials say privately that, if only the West (that is, America) would help both countries and persuade China to stop its war dance, the Vietnamese army will go home.

Up to last month, Vietnam had sent to Cambodia 10,000 tons of rice seed, 20,000 tons of rice, 9,000 tons of fuel and 5,000 tons of consumer goods, such as condensed milk. The Vietnamese have managed to divide that 'one grain of salt' by coupling their provinces with provinces in Cambodia. For example, Kompong Speu has been 'adopted' by Cuu Long province, where every Vietnamese family is being asked to contribute three kilogrammes of rice. At the hospital at Kompong Speu, we happened on a line of several hundred people receiving rice that had just arrived from Saigon. According to a nurse at this hospital, the International Red Cross has given 'some instruments, which are very useful... that's all.'

Britain, whose Prime Minister has been especially shrill on South East Asian affairs this year, is sending *nothing* to Cambodia. Some £425,000 has been promised as part of an EEC development grant to the United Nations High Commissioner on Refugees, and this will go to refugees. Mrs Thatcher has suspended all food relief aid to Vietnam, Cambodia's *only* life-line.

The British Minister for 'overseas aid' is now directly responsible to the Foreign Office. His name is Neil Marten and when an *Oxford Mail* reporter telephoned him last week following my reports in the *Daily Mirror,* he said this: 'The Government will be helping through the International Red Cross. One of the objections (to giving aid to Cambodia) is that the Vietnamese are preventing it from getting in and their inability to get it distributed. The Red Cross is doing what they can, but they don't seem to be getting much help through. Anyway, the

situation in Cambodia is all Vietnam's fault!' What is important about the
Minister's statement is that almost all of it is untrue.

In the suburbs of Phnom Penh there is an extermination centre where the
Khmer Rouge tortured and killed 12,000 people. Like the Nazis, they photographed their victims before and after they hanged them, slit their throats,
drowned them, beat them to death and electrocuted them. Like at Auschwitz,
there is a room filled with clothes, many of them children's. The Khmer Rouge
were the most thorough mass murderers since Hitler.

Perhaps it is shameful enough that Britain still recognises the defunct Khmer
Rouge 'government'. That the British and other governments should deny
humanitarian aid to the survivors, who are starving, diminishes us all. As I have
mentioned, they are mostly children.

(21 September 1979)

The 'filthy affair' of denying relief
John Pilger

Early in October 1979, the International Committee of the Red Cross telexed the New Statesman to say that it wished to 'withdraw' a letter for publication which had been intended to follow my Cambodia report on 21 September. The letter, signed by Alain Moudoux, head of public relations in Geneva, had merely protested the ICRC's 'neutrality'—that is, its insistence on supplying the Khmer Rouge as a pre-condition to mounting a relief programme for most of the population—and confirmed that only 100 tons of relief (or, as M. Moudoux put it, 'more than' 100 tons) had been sent by Geneva to Phnom Penh: in effect, virtually nothing.

The withdrawal of the letter is perhaps symptomatic of the debilitating malaise affecting both the world's leading international relief agencies, the ICRC and the United Nations Children's Fund, UNICEF. Cambodia has traumatised them; their spokesmen no longer know what to say, for what can they say? While every day hundreds of Khmer children die from lack of the simplest things—powdered milk, rice, antibiotics, vitamins, anti-malarials—the bureaucracies of the two agencies struggle to cover their inaction and to create the illusion that they are doing something.

For example, the ICRC's announcement on 27 September 1979 that the Phnom Penh government had acceded to its 'programme' was a deception, aimed, no doubt, at forcing the Cambodian authorities to accept the seemingly endless caravan of conditions, guarantees, political strings etc., that would roll into Cambodia behind the 'neutral' services of the Red Cross. What it did force was an official denial from Phnom Penh and a shoring up of the deeply felt suspicion, in both Cambodia and Vietnam, that the ICRC and UNICEF represent not humanitarianism, but a Trojan horse.

This is a justifiable fear, because the culpable denial of relief by the international agencies—culpable, because they have representatives in Cambodia who report the daily spectacle of death—accurately reflects the twisted politics of the West toward Cambodia. The aim of these politics is, as the *Guardian* outlined in a perceptive leader on 25 September, '... to structure aid to Cambodia in such a way as to give minimum legitimacy to Heng Samrin (the Phnom Penh government) and maximum help to Pol Pot... and to pursue the unrealistic aim of using an army of aid officials in Cambodia as a means of "internationalising" that country and opening it up to Sihanouk'. In the *Observer,* Brian Eads, the paper's Bangkok correspondent, quoted a relief official as saying that the ICRC and UNICEF 'want absolute licence, a radio station, diplomatic status. They want powers and assurances that would make them more powerful than the Government in Phnom Penh. It's easy to see how this is unacceptable!'

On the surface, the ICRC's major demand—that it be permitted to supply what is left of the Khmer Rouge—might seem reasonable on strictly humanitarian grounds. But in practice it is as much a fiction as the United Nations' 'recognition' of a non-existent Pol Pot regime; and the ICRC knows it. When I asked a senior ICRC man in Geneva if the Khmer Rouge had agreed to *all* the demands imposed on Phnom Penh, he replied, 'No, of course not. We would have to do pretty much as we're doing now: drop the stuff over the Thai border and get out quickly'. Those who have glimpsed the Khmer Rouge camps confirm that 'dropped' food is not reaching the people, but feeding the Khmer Rouge 'black shirts', the most enduring fanatics of Pol Pot's army of genocide. (These murderers are the 'government' to which Britain gave its vote at the United Nations.)

One of the most anaemic excuses for not mounting an aid programme—that food might be syphoned off to the Vietnamese army—has been abandoned, probably because tales of Vietnamese soldiers harassing supply convoys (dispensed mostly by the US Embassy in Bangkok) have never been substantiated. Jacques Danois, a senior UNICEF man in Bangkok, said, 'These stories are unfounded. The distribution is very satisfactory. We do have control of the relief and we are convinced that it is reaching civilians'. Then *why* don't the agencies scuttle their transparently political conditions and get on with saving the Khmer people from the extinction?

The answer lies in the obvious. Most of UNICEF's budget comes from the US Government and UNICEF and the ICRC have jointly formulated their grounded Cambodia operation. For all its pretensions of neutrality, the Red Cross depends on mostly Western exchequers for its funds. 'If we run counter to the interests of certain governments', the ICRC official told me, 'we run the risk of not getting any money'. This is only half true; the timorous nature of the ICRC bureaucracy is also a major factor. If Geneva simply decided to go ahead and to save lives, public opinion in Western countries would support its efforts and the politicians would follow. The British Government has now announced that it will give £4 million to Cambodia, mostly via the ICRC and UNICEF, and public opinion was undoubtedly the catalyst.

Lord Carrington's announcement of the £4 million followed a press conference in Geneva at which the ICRC and UNICEF launched an appeal to governments for £50 million for Cambodia. The British contribution is, of course, splendid; but will it get there? Or, perhaps more to the point, is it merely a gesture? The answer to this question is paramount, because there is a disquieting side to the ICRC 'appeal'. There has been no indication that the relief agencies have modified their intransigence on the conditions I have outlined, or that any agreement has been reached with Phnom Penh. I put this to a veteran relief agency official, who has followed the Cambodia tragedy with deepening melancholy. He said: 'We are holding our breath. The Red Cross and UNICEF are going ahead, fully aware of the obstruction that lies ahead and that it is of their making. They also know that *they* are causing attitudes to harden in Phnom Penh and that there is the possibility of a confrontation; what they are trying on is "gunboat relief". It's

Eric Piper/Syndication International

Khmer Rouge receive the West's largesse at Sa Kaeo camp on the Thai border.

so damned cynical. There are even breathless stories in Geneva about the possibility of "our planes being shot at". I pray that all this is not true, that an informal
agreement we don't know about has been reached. But I have to say that in all the
years I have been in the business of helping people in distress, I have never known
such a filthy affair'.

The purely political question of who is seen to be governing Cambodia remains
at the root of why the relief agencies have pursued the fiction of 'two sides' and
have allowed thousands to starve during the three months since the Phnom Penh
government appealed for relief. (A whole month passed before the ICRC
replied.) In 1970 Western governments rushed to recognise the Lon Nol military
regime, even though it administered only the towns and highways, because Lon
Nol complied with the West's (that is, America's) strategic interests in the region.
The relief agencies followed suit. The Heng Samrin government administers the
towns, the highways and most of the countryside. But the West, in defiance of the
tradition of basing recognition on the control of territory, refuses even de facto
recognition, because it was brought to power with help from Vietnam. As Evan
Luard, a member of the UN Human Rights Commission, pointed out in the
Guardian last week: 'When another brutal regime was overthrown in an exactly
similar way in Uganda earlier this year we (and the UN) recognised it immediately, even while foreign forces remained on Ugandan soil and while fighting
continued.'   One of the most depressing aspects to this 'filthy affair' is the
inexorable drift back to an atmosphere similar to that which burdened South East
Asia in the early Sixties. Under the here-we-go-again headline, UNCLE SAM
ARMS THE THAIS, the current *Newsweek* reports:

> The US is pouring arms into Thailand... Washington's arms sales to Bangkok
> add up to 400 million dollars so far this year, about four times the average of
> recent years. The Pentagon is jumping Thailand to the head of the line for
> deliveries of N-48 Patton tanks, anti-tank missiles, mortars and M-16 rifles.

Of course, the difference between the 1960s and 1979 is that America has a new
and powerful friend in the region, China. From 23 October the airspace over the
Gulf of Tonkin will be 'dangerous', according to a Peking announcement. The
Chinese are conducting naval and air manoeuvres within sight of Haiphong,
Vietnam's most important port and its only intact industrial centre. The Vietnamese expect a Chinese attack from the sea at the end of the month. Once again,
they are beleaguered, militarily and economically. If they pull out of Cambodia,
they will be exposed on the west and the Chinese surely will try to re-install Pol
Pot; if they stay in Cambodia, they will be outlawed internationally and the West's
embargo on them will continue to have the precise effect of forcing them deeper
into the arms of the Soviet Union.

Last week Robert MacNamara, the head of the World Bank, said that political
strings demanded by the American government were preventing food aid from
reaching one and a quarter million people throughout the world. He made special
mention of Vietnam which, although itself on the edge of famine, is also attempting to feed Cambodia. Coming from MacNamara, a former Defence Secretary
and an LBJ hawk, this statement has particular credibility and confirms the
effectiveness of the most powerful weapon in America's armoury: the denial of
food. And nowhere is that weapon more lethal than in once deliciously obscure
and bountiful Cambodia, whose neutrality was destroyed by American bombs.

I have been working in a film editing room above Berwick Street in Soho watching some of the 12 hours of footage which director David Munro and I brought back from Cambodia for an ATV documentary (and which, incidentally, the ACTT have given us dispensation to make). The images of dying, crying starving children are so horrific that I suggested that viewers may not be able to 'take it': that we should delete some of them. But we are not going to do that; for those eyes set in faces that are almost skulls, which still bring tears to those of us who filmed them, will indict every accessory to their preventable death: every relief agency man who makes his craven excuses for doing nothing, every impeccable politician and foreign policy bureaucrat who never sees such children and participates, in however minor a role, in the 'filthy affair' that is the denial of food and medicines for political reasons. All the children in our film can now be presumed dead.

(12 October 1979)

A time for pragmatic marriage
Anthony Barnett

Cambodia is coming back to life. The sense of growth is palpable, especially in Phnom Penh, which now has over a quarter of a million inhabitants. Its degree of normalisation, which is not reflected in the provinces, is far from complete, but nonetheless impressive. The city's January 7th Hospital had a death rate for adult admissions of 13 per cent in November 1979. Now it is only 3 per cent. What is occurring is so new, in circumstances so unparalleled, that it is impossible to predict the outcome. Certainly Cambodia is vulnerable, like a young plant pushing its way above ground. What will happen if the elements are harsh and unremitting has yet to be seen. Violence could easily destroy it. Will the Vietnamese shield, which has so far protected it, also cut out the sun and stunt the growth it has made possible?

The Heng Samrin administration wants to dissociate itself in every way it can from Pol Pot's. A regime of forced labour, of directed residence, without religion, or trade or a school system, has been replaced by one of uncoerced labour, decontrolled residence, religious observation, free individual exchange and a significant education programme. But the most peculiar hallmark of Pol Pot has yet to be reversed: there is still no Cambodian money. Putting banknotes into circulation proved much more complicated than having them printed last year.

The new national currency will have to replace, if it can, five others: the dollar, gold, rice, the Vietnamese dong and the Thai bhat. A lot of trade is taking place with these as the medium of exchange. Both the Vietnamese and Thai borders have been open to the peasant trader. There is a trans-Cambodian bicycle trail. (The whole journey takes about a week: some of the more enterprising Khmer are buying US goods in Thailand, shipping them to South Vietnam, and undoubtedly taking a good profit.) All along the roads there is a steady line of operators, hauling in textiles and cigarettes from the West; bikes, hats and domestic goods from the East.

Never hold gold in contempt. The recent feverish buying of the useless metal on the international exchanges is not without its rationality. Centuries of accumulation have held the Cambodian peasant in good stead. In 1975, when the forced exodus took place, tiny packets were hidden about the bodies of those on the road. Many were buried on the way, and lost. But a large proportion of the evacuees made it back to the village in which they were born or had close relatives, before they were moved on to work-sites. The packets were handed over and buried. No doubt they were one of the reasons why everybody returned to the villages once more, walking across Cambodia, immediately Pol Pot was overthrown. The bikes, the new sarongs, are not the result of aid. They have been bought by Cambodians themselves. Today, in one of Phnom Penh's markets you can pick up, as I did, a pair of J 'King of Freedom' Jeans, from a stall table, with old women gossiping across it. But I had to put them back, I couldn't meet the price. They could only be acquired with the yellow metal, which until now I'd always held in contempt.

Without doubt the Vietnamese-supported administration was in no position to close the borders. It had the military strength, but not the economic leverage to provide the badly needed items, or the food which was also being shipped in from Thailand. But it is difficult to see how a new currency can be introduced into an economy without frontiers. Thus, while the circulation of Cambodian paper will undoubtedly be welcomed by the people, it will almost certainly be necessary to curtail the Thai trade routes, and this will not be popular, especially not with the petty merchants who already dominate exchange.

All the officials I asked were evasive about when money would be introduced. 'Sometime this year' was the general answer. But it seems the administration is hoping to introduce a whole package of measures, dramatically, to underline its legitimacy and its voereignty. The big central market in Phnom Penh is being done up, its layered dome interior repainted. A symbol of the capital's role as a trading centre, it has still be be opened. A new Constitution is being drafted to replace the revolutionary council with a proper state protocol and legal system. Postage stamps have been designed. All may be introduced in time for the Cambodian new year—in April.*

Soon after that, the rains will begin, movement along the roads, which are in awful condition, will become more difficult, all hands will be needed to plough the fields and plant the rice. While the introduction of money is a crucial test facing the administration in its political and economic consolidation, another, more critical struggle will be to get the main harvest planted. If it is not, if Pol Pot attacks the countryside, with his Chinese arms and American patronage, then another disaster will follow. The international agencies recognise that aid has to be brought in this year, to make up for the shortfall. Next year, their budgets will not allow them to be so forthcoming. Cambodia at present is suffering an acutely harsh dry season, which has brought a very small intermediate harvest. The main crops, which are planted as waters begin to rise and harvested towards the end of the year, will be the key. They will have to provide for the subsequent months, in what has been and should be a surplus-producing country. As one of the most able and energetic of the international experts working in Phnom Penh put it, Cambodia in the coming seasons might hope to reach the level of an underdeveloped country; only then, could one begin to think about development.

Cambodia's present problems evidently do not have a single cause. The discrepancy between town and country (which is being recreated at the moment) stretches back to Sihanouk. The catastrophe of the American war, which pulverised the countryside and completed the corruption and demoralisation of the elite, is still recent history, which ended only five years ago. The Pol Pot regime imposed its brutal folly on the population, and became increasingly violent and indiscrimi-

---

* The currency was indeed introduced in April 1980.

nate in its use of terror. Finally, his overthrow brought its own train of destruction and terrible economic dislocation. The consequences of this violently layered past differ sharply from region to region. There are no reliable statistics. There are many zones of insecurity, shrouded in secrecy.

The total population is probably close to five million. Experts (if such there can be about today's Cambodia) reckon, for example, that the population of Kompong Cham, the most numerous province, is close to 700,000, compared with nearly a million in 1970. Battambang has about 600,000 inhabitants, down from nearly 700,000 at the end of the 1960s. If the figures for these two provinces were based on the claims of each local administration they would be over one million and close to 850,000 respectively. Extended over the whole country, such levels would put the total up to between 7 and 8 million—certainly far too high. One immediately sees the sort of problem aid agencies and indeed the central administration faces. From the province to the hamlet, people will tend to exaggerate numbers in order to obtain more supplies. Major population losses seem to have taken place in Kompot, Svay Rieng and Kratie. It is now well authenticated that the Pol Pot regime in its last year deported the vast part of the population in the eastern provinces, close to Vietnam, to the interior. Many of them were then killed in mass executions. A mounting number of the so-called 'new people', who were deported from the cities in 1975, were also killed in villages across the whole country. But 'old people', that is peasants who remained in the areas 'liberated' by Pol Pot before he captured Phnom Penh in 1975, do not seem to have been killed indiscriminately—although they were subject to punitive execution.

It was Pol Pot's policy to build a greater Cambodia, 'at great leap forward pace', to cite his own hardly original formulation, but his regime did not set out to exterminate everybody. To say this is not to grant him very much, but helps to explain why so many and so much have survived, however broken or vandalised. The ratio of men to women, the absence of children between one and six, have been remarked upon, but not measured. There are orphanages, where there were not before. There are not myriads of small infants on the verge of real childhood, as in other Asian countries. Most of the women in the factories are widows. If the demographic trends of the 1950s and 1960s had continued in Cambodia through the 1970s, as they did in neighbouring lands, there would now be around ten million Cambodians.

At present the population is eating, but not enough. Anaemia, rather than starvation, is the major problem. In two months' time existing food stocks will run out over much of the country. Unless food aid is more widely distributed, seed rice will prbobably be consumed in its place, thus reproducing the cycle of shortages and famine.

Everybody in the aid organisations seems to agree that once rice gets to the level of the Srok, or district, or below, to the villages and hamlets, it is fairly equitably and effectively handed out, as families come in with their ox-carts to collect their share. But getting the rice to the place of final distribution is not easy, and there must still be many villages which have not received aid, or have only seen derisory amounts, since mid-1979.

Before then, the Vietnamese army distributed rice, much of it from its own meagre rations. Had it not done so, there would have been widespread deaths, it is said. One Cambodian told me that the hunger was bad, and that in a fairly remote hamlet in Eastern Kompong Cham he received 50 kilograms of rice aid in mid-1979. Ironically, and tellingly perhaps, he believed it was from the International

Red Cross; at the time no Western aid had reached the country. A more precise acknowledgement came from a doctor at the Phnom Penh orphanage, who said that food was first delivered by the Vietnamese 24th Infantry Brigade.

But some time around August-September 1979, the Hanoi Army handed over distribution to the new administration. The first civilian convoy took days to travel nervously along the roads, as its drivers felt their way into unknown terrain. The creation of a Cambodian distribution network involves five things. First, the technical means, from lorries to bridges, to deliver aid at all. Second, it involves logistical organisation, from maintenance to bookkeeping: knowing where lorries are, getting fuel, putting convoys together, ranking drivers, etc. Third, a considerable administrative capacity is needed, to decide priorities, distinguish between provincial claims, send notification of decisions. In both technical organisation and political administration the new regime was extremely inexperienced. Raw, young, shaken and cautious. In a country of extreme scarcity the value of a few bags of rice off the back of a lorry is enormous. Thus, fourth, a system of controlling distribution and preventing theft, however bureaucratic and time-consuming, is evidently necessary. Finally, there is the need for leadership, to get everyone—from the dockers who are supposed to unload in the hot February sun, to the drivers who must bump their way across perilous bridges, to the pen pushers—to work really hard.

The advance in the country's technical distribution capacity has been considerable, from a rock-bottom starting point. In October 1979 there was a total of between 100 and 200 functioning lorries in Cambodia, mostly of Chinese manufacture. They were all that were left over from Pol Pot—thanks to his military strategy of rapid retreat before the Vietnamese main force. Photographs of the old regime's base close to the Thai border, at which the Vietnamese captured Ieng Sary's Chinese passport, show a camp strewn with wrecked trucks.

Today there are now close on 1,200 lorries at the disposal of the administration (compared with 10,000 before Sihanouk was ousted). Malcolm Harper of Oxfam reckons another 1,000 lorries are needed to get the food to the outer villages. The country has extensive waterways and UNICEF is bringing in tugs, barges and motorised barges. Oxfam is hoping to bring in some ferries which will rapidly speed up the crossing time of the Mekong for aid lorries.

The most striking improvement in the country's distribution capacity has been made without the help of western agencies. The railway line from Phnom Penh to Battambang, sabotaged by Pol Pot's forces as they retreated, is now open again, its bridges repaired. In two days, a train load of between 500 and 1,000 tons can reach one of the main rice-growing areas of Cambodia. Battambang needs 20,000 tons of seed rice by April, an almost impossible target for transportation along 300 kilometres of smashed road. Battambang's harvest may well be the key to success or failure in 1980, but getting the seed rice there is not the only obstacle. Few of the tractors in the area are functioning, and many of the draft animals have foot and mouth disease, while the local administration lacks the means of preventative innoculation.

In Kompong Speu, just off the country's only good road, which is also the main aid artery from the port of Kompong Som to Phnom Penh, the provincial hospital is in poor shape. It has no running water, and no mechanised water delivery. It has no qualified doctor, and the nurse who is in charge seems somewhat overwhelmed. Some of the wards housing its 250 patients still have no beds. Nobody seemed to know the present mortality rate. The contrasts in this hospital of huts were very sharp. The province is famous for its sugar palms, and in the grounds an agile, splendidly muscled man, with slightly graying hair, was nimbly mounting the tall trees to collect the sweet brown juice in his bamboo containers. In the maternity ward a woman had just successfully delivered twins: the aura and exhilaration of childbirth was about her, it seems universal. When people know what they are doing, they can do it to the full. The medical staff, on the other hand, seemed out of their depth and demoralised. All they could do was ask for help.

There is an avid desire for schooling among Khmer youth, after the years of agricultural labour, when children worked the fields. UNICEF officials accept that at least 700,000 children are in classes, however rudimentary. Every village has set up a school of some sort. One can see 'open classes', from the road, in the grounds of vandalised pagodas, and the figure of 35,000 at school in Phnom Penh seems quite plausible—children with plastic satchels are a common sight. However, there is virtually no secondary education in the country, because a whole generation has missed its initial formation. Will those who had no education during the war against America and then the Pol Pot years be able to catch up, or will they be permanently disabled?

One of the strangest things about Cambodia is the juxtaposition of Phnom Penh and the surrounding countryside. No real active relationship yet exists between the two. In part this is a problem inherited from the Sihanouk years. The vandalism, the shattered buildings, the gutted remains of villas that have been fired by the impromptu cooking of new inhabitants, make the city look like parts of Eastside New York. Despite this the town retains a stunning beauty, its wide, tree-lined avenues are more modern and less worn than Hanoi's. A great deal of recent building remains, including fine houses, hotels, and government offices, many of them far better furnished than in the Vietnamese capital.

The wealth which built this city, which had barely 100,000 inhabitants before the Second World War, most of them Chinese and Vietnamese, was extracted from the countryside. Every provincial governor had his Phnom Penh villa, for example. With the exception of the French-owned rubber plantations, Cambodia had no concentrated natural resource, such as oil, to fund the modern construction work. One of the reasons for the hatred of the city, displayed by the poor peasants of Cambodia and exploited by Pol Pot, stemmed from its onerous impact on the countryside. Usury and corruption extracted the rural surplus, drove peasants into debt, and for the first time created a significant landless class in a country which is relatively underpopulated. Two of the younger officials I spoke with, now holding significant posts under Heng Samrin, came from landless, peasant families.

A comparison with Vietnam is instructive, as it indicates some of the problems which lie ahead. Phnom Penh is not like Saigon, which was created in its present form (with still over two and a half million inhabitants) by a vast infusion of American largesse. The US war helped to preserve Phnom Penh as an island apart from its surrounding countryside. And across the countryside the US air assault helped to destroy what wealth there was in the villages. Oxfam set out to count the number of intact brick or concrete buildings in rural areas across Cambodia, and gave up when they found none. Primarily, this is the legacy of US bombing.

In North Vietnam, the contrast between town and city is simply the reverse of what was the Cambodian relationship. Hanoi is worn, tremendously overcrowded and starved of construction and housing projects. But the countryside is wealthy with accumulated savings, and brick houses are going up everywhere; there is far

Anthony Barnett

Phnom Penh markets, February 1980 (above) and August 1981 (below)—glossy consumer goods from Thailand appeared within 18 months.

Anthony Barnett

more living space and more food. The Vietnamese leadership relied upon the political commitment, and unity, of the urban elite to follow Ho Chi Minh's patriotic socialism and sacrifice its material deserts. This enabled it to follow a relatively relaxed policy towards the peasantry, without forcible extraction.

It seems inconceivable that a similar pattern could now be reproduced in Cambodia. Even the *laissez-faire* policy adopted towards Saigon will not be applicable in Phnom Penh. To stabilise an administration there, in today's conditions, demands the rapid creation of a level of urban life that in turn means a pattern of consumption considerably better than in the countryside. Already the legal rations of the Phnom Penh functionaries have outstripped those of Hanoi. Last week all employees in one major ministry were given five generously sized tins of Hungarian goulash and some Hungarian cigarettes: wealth indeed, but small compensation for the tension and insecurity of working in Phnom Penh.

Weddings are another source of additional rations, and they give a revealing glimpse of life in Phnom Penh today. A lot of people are getting married. One young man I spoke to had taken a wife three months ago at the suggestion of distant relatives—all he had left. They brought together two orphans, so that they would at least have family support from each other. He seemed pleased with the arrangement. At the same time the marriage released food into the community, from the employer—inevitably a government ministry. I attended one wedding of a couple who are nurses in the dispensary run by the Ministry of Foreign Affairs. (This itself is significant. Each Ministry protects its own, and provides a GP service, for a staff chronically prone to illness.) The two announced their intention to their Ministry, which then arranged everything. The Pol Pot regime banned romance and even directed marriages in group ceremonies. So the new government has made the benediction of free unions one of its strong points.

The ministry lays on a substantial feast. There were over 200 people present at the celebration with soups, meats, fish paté and plenty of rice as well as a pineapple wine recently manufactured in the alcohol factory. There was a large band, electric guitars and traditional drums, and traditional as well as western dancing. Such celebrations continue well into the small hours, despite the fact that there is a curfew at 9.00. The one I attended was interrupted by a city-wide power cut, at 8pm: 'Bad luck for the marriage', I was told, with traditional Khmer fatalism. The same night there was another wedding at the Ministry of Fisheries. Someone with reasonable connections could attend one a week. Obviously, it is wasteful and unfair to duplicate a complete medical dispensary in every ministry when provincial hospitals can lack almost everything, and to provide largesse to those already in receipt of a reasonable ration, when there are villagers with much less only a day's drive away. On the other hand, the security and reassurance provided, however strained, is a priority to stabilise the administration—the very people whose sense of purpose is needed to get the aid lorries moving at all. Despite the government's efforts, there is a constant haemorrhage of the surviving elite (French-speaking in the main, but with a surprising amount of English) to Thailand and the West.

Provided that Phnom Penh's wealth comes from aid, especially from the Communist bloc, consumer goods and a wide range of foods will not depress the standard of living in the countryside. Nonetheless, it is in the countryside that productive investment is most needed. There are forty factories now operating in Phnom Penh, with an average of over a hundred employees. It is policy to encourage artisan production, from sewing to bike repairs. But it will be some time before such activities can hope to produce enough to support a population of nearly 300,000.

Pol Pot declared that the countryside would be turned into a 'checker-board' of vast square irrigation canals, with a regular square field system in between. And it has been. The rural panorama is a monotonous pattern of right-angled lines, and square paddy fields, from the road, from the air, in province after province. A country where there was little irrigation before now has plenty. Too much, people say, as many of the canals are useless. To realise that the endless earthworks were thrown up in only three years, during the dry season when the earth was hardening and the sun was very hot, is to see how the people groaned. Two cubic metres a day was the minimum requirement, to receive a ration of thin rice gruel. The big fields certainly grew rice, which was stored in impressive brick and timber granaries. But the ubiquity of complaints about the rations, full of graphic detail, make it beyond doubt that large sections of the population suffered cruelly not only from forced labour, but also from a deliberately inadequate diet: the precondition for Pol Pot's brilliant achievement of exporting rice.

Richard Dudman, a correspondent for the St Louis *Post Dispatch*, who was one of the few Western journalists to visit Pol Pot's Democratic Kampuchea, concluded that 'one of the world's great housing programmes' was under way. There was indeed some building. Brick kilns from the Pol Pot years can be seen in Kompong Cham. There is a Pol Pot housing estate on the road to Kompong Speu. The houses are small and grouped together in straight lines, again like the 'checker-board', which is in sharp contrast to the dispersed arrangements of traditional Khmer habitation. Dudman praised the way concrete bases were being used to support the stilts of the houses, raised above the annual flood level. But Cambodians I spoke to insisted that this was an innovation of the Sihanouk years.

Who will now own the land? Peasants have begun to farm small private plots. Freshly constructed but very primitive bamboo and wattle huts are surrounded by newly sown vegetables, especially along the Mekong where there is water. But the paddy fields themselves are being worked by production solidarity teams, on a co-operative basis. There is no evidence that land will be distributed. Rather, the collectivisation of the fields will probably be preserved by the new Cambodian government, with their control passing from the national state to village level. How the peasants themselves respond to this new system will be critical in determining the level of rice production. People say that 'the Cambodians do not want socialism'. But they usually refer to members of the elite already trained in Western ways who show a marked resistence to collective enterprise. It is impossible to establish through an interpreter, in present circumstances, before planting has begun, how the villages and hamlets will respond. Will they support Phnom Penh, if the city continues to be relatively unproductive?

The last harvest may have been very small, but for perhaps the first time in living memory it was not subject to expropriation. A major incentive to peasant labour, the absence of taxation will not enrich the towns if it continues as policy. Then, the still visible splendours of old Phnom Penh may seem to rebuke the new inhabitants for their penury.

In many ways the relationship between the city and the countryside defines the quality and values of every society, and determines its stability and growth. Behind the recent history of Cambodia's terrible suffering lies a long tradition of extreme imbalance and inequality between urban and rural life. The French peopled the towns with Chinese and Vietnamese. Sihanouk redoubled the colonial rate of extraction from the peasantry. The Americans cut off Phnom Penh with air power. Pol Pot emptied it completely. Today the capital is still an urban island. It is no longer empty or inactive but it remains as tense as a forced smile. The long-term reconstruction in Cambodia demands something quite new in its history: to replace a relationship of antagonism and exploitation with a balanced affinity between Phnom Penh and a land well endowed with sun and water.

(14 March 1980)

Between Vietnam and Pol Pot
Anthony Barnett

Cambodians do not say they were liberated by the Vietnamese, but they speak without strain or falseness of their liberation, and they know what made this possible. At present the Vietnamese army is accepted, as a fact of life and as a massive guard against the return of Pol Pot. Unarmed Vietnamese mingle in the markets, lone Vietnamese soldiers can be seen on foot patrol in a road full of Khmer on bikes—inconceivable if there were active hostility between the two peoples. But it is clear that the Vietnamese feel themselves to be foreigners, in a strange land; they are extremely nervous in their relations with Khmer. On the whole Cambodians treat the Vietnamese with caution. In private each will circulate horror stories of the other. When one sees two Vietnamese soldiers biking unarmed down a street in Phnom Penh, one pedalling, the other sitting sideways on the pillion, one sees men from a peasant army. Each wishes 'to return as soon as possible to his country, to his native village', Le Duc Tho said in December 1979. Whether they wish it or not it is absolutely evident that they need to return as soon as possible, for Vietnam needs its sons. The meagreness of Vietnam's resources makes its achievement in Cambodia all the more remarkable and impressive.

The Vietnamese who are in Cambodia are by no means a homogeneous group. There are the soldiers and their officers—certainly more than 200,000 stationed throughout the populated areas. They say they are engaged in a police operation. If so, it is a very large one. The prime aim of the Vietnamese army seems to be to provide reassurance that the present order is here to stay. At the same time, it is said, the Vietnamese themselves are not so permanent. Second, there are the advisers, observing, training and persuading their younger Cambodian counterparts; how far they are felt to be giving instructions still, it is impossible to judge. Third, there are the 'cowboys', lorry drivers in their Dodge trucks, working the roads. Some under contract to the Cambodian government, US-trained, they are the Vietnamese equivalent of the small private air companies, saved from bankruptcy by the Cambodian aid bonanza. Finally, there are Vietnamese specialists, working in Phnom Penh from the hotel service to the hospital.

Have the Vietnamese been involved in looting and plunder? No one could speak for the cowboys. (There can be little doubt that Phnom Penh was stripped of many consumer goods, especially TV sets.) Aid personnel who have lived in the country for months, and who have developed working relationships with Cambodians, are adamant that stories of Vietnamese atrocities and pillage are manufactured in Thailand, or elsewhere. Rice supplies for Vietnamese troops come into Kompong Som on Vietnamese Army boats, and are unloaded by soldiers into army trucks, on a regular basis. I spoke to one Cambodian who wanted to join his family in Europe and evidently disliked foreign domination. Wearing a new digital watch, he claimed there was Vietnamese corruption. Where? 'In the countryside', he claimed, which seemed unlikely. Did he not then prefer Pol Pot? 'The Vietnamese do not genocide people' was his matter-of-fact response.

The factory machinery now in use in Phnom Penh is evidence that Vietnam's official policy is not how it has been painted in the West. The plastics factory, which Oxfam has put back into operation, is full of presses that mould useful consumer items for which there is a high demand in Vietnam. Its tool shop has Korean drills and lathes. In the canned-milk factory there is a good supply of tinplate, from the Lon Nol period. It would have been easy for the Vietnamese to have hoisted such valuables on to a lorry. They would have been immensely more precious than many tons of rice, because it is precisely in return for consumer goods that the Vietnamese peasants will deliver rice to the towns. By contrast, French officials in Hanoi confirmed that the new anis plant which was set up in Lang Son with French government aid, by an agreement in 1976, had all its machinery removed by the invading Chinese army, which then levelled the freshly built factory with dynamite.

Far from entering a colonial venture of profitable exploitation, the Vietnamese authorities, it seems, recognised that they would have to pay, economically and politically, when they ordered their troops into Cambodia. What is their strategic objective? In his December 1979 statement, Le Duc Tho simply said that three offers to negotiate were turned down while Pol Pot attacks continued, leaving Vietnam with 'no alternative' than to fight back. 'Our counter-attacks on the Pol Pot-Ieng Sary army were not simply an act of self-defence, but also a contribution to the liberation of the Kampuchean people from the Pol Pot-Ieng Sary genocidal regime, as desired by them.' Only then does he go on to discuss the Cambodian resistance, and concludes: 'Any honest and clear-sighted Kampuchean will approve of the aid given by our army to their people in their struggle for self-liberation.'

With this formula Hanoi formally recognises that liberation cannot simply be delivered to others, but that they must gain it for themselves. Nevertheless, the Vietnamese army has remained in Cambodia, and will do so until the threat from China ends, they say. Will the continued presence of the Vietnamese in Cambodia undermine their objective of creating an authentically friendly regime there? While a precipitate withdrawal would generate another human disaster, the more rapidly the Vietnamese pull out the more likely they are to leave behind a fraternal state. Chinese policy, therefore, is to pin down the Vietnamese: 'It is wise for China to force the Vietnamese to stay in Cambodia because that way they will suffer more and more', Deng Xiaoping told Japanese Premiere Ohira last year,[*] revealing most exactly his feelings for the Cambodian people themselves.

At least four significant groups can be distinguished in the new Cambodian administration. There are the top government officials, the ministers, generals and political directors of the regime. There are the technical advisers, factory

---

[*] Cited in the *Far Eastern Economic Review,* 21 December 1979.

managers, and other officials left over from the Sihanouk and Lon Nol years who are not socialists, and are unlikely to become so. There are the relatively young administrators who are socialists, many of whom were students in the Lon Nol period, and are still in their twenties. These men, already in positions of consider-able responsibility for their age, represent the backbone for any future left-wing regime. They were not formed in Vietnam—that generation is largely dead—but in the last year most have been there for crash-study courses. Finally, there are the new soldiers of the regime: the army, the local militia and the police.

The number of armed Cambodians attached to the Heng Samrin state seems surprisingly large. I was not able to get any figures from officials. But armed Khmer can be seen everywhere and on independent as well as joint patrols. the military effectiveness of a young, inexperienced and relatively casual force must leave a lot to be desired. They would not yet be an adequate answer to Pol Pot. Nonetheless, it must make a difference to the populace that Khmer are carrying arms. These are often ill-assorted. When we visited the mass grave by the broken television station in Phnom Penh, two Khmer girls wandered up with American M-16s over their shoulders. Vietnamese officials place much stress on the Khmer armed forces, their strength and speed of development. They seem to see this as the key to stabilising the country's new administration.

Heng Samrin is apparently a pleasant and sincere man, but he is evidently somewhat retiring and uncharismatic. Pen Sovan, the Vice-President, whose photo can be seen alongside Heng Samrin's, was an early defector from the Pol Pot movement, before it seized power. He had joined the Vietminh in 1950, as a boy. The third-ranking member of the administration, Chea Sim, who heads the Ministry of the Interior, is a large man with an amiable style which exudes warmth and a rare sense of self-confidence. But his public role seems limited to silent appearances. No one in the leadership speaks well in public or has expressed the sentiments of recovery from the past in a way that evidently echoes the feeling of the people.

One of the aid officials said to me that he just couldn't understand why young Khmer did not say 'Thank you very much' to the Vietnamese for liberating them, welcome the opportunity to rebuild their country, roll up their sleeves and get to it. 'Why aren't they feeling happy at least about trying?' he asked.

There is definitely an unease as well as some incompetence among the Cambo-dian administrators; a mixture of fatalism and resignation afflicts some of the technical officials who speak Western languages. And this is rooted in the recent Cambodian experience. To see why, some understanding of Pol Pot is essential. For although he is now presented as a stooge of the Chinese, and there is no denying his having fallen into the arms of Chinese advisers, he was and remains a Khmer nationalist. Sihanouk was a vicious joke for many of the elite, and he ran his administration with considerable French aid (documents of the Sihanouk period, preserved in the national archives, were in French not Khmer). The Prince was followed by Lon Nol, who then 'invited' Saigon troops to help him and was protected by US bombing. Lon Nol was overthrown by what was finally an indigenous and independent Cambodian force—led by Pol Pot. In a major speech of September 1977, outlining the Party history, Pol Pot declared that his Cambo-dia was 100 per cent independent: politically, militarily, economically and even culturally. You can't get more 'independent' than that.

One Heng Samrin official made the reasonable estimate that perhaps one-ninth of the population would have said they supported him in 1978. These supporters, however, were Khmer, not Chinese, even if it was the latter who supplied the guns. The black-pyjamaed Brigade leaders and the executioners (who were poor peasants) were also Cambodians. This is not an easy fact to assimilate, when one is trying to re-establish a new national state, and assert its independence. It has to be something less than Pol Pot's.

It would have been easier to assimilate the *national* meaning of having thrown up such a monstrous regime, if it had been capably opposed from the beginning. Here is surely the most demoralising fact of all, especially for Cambodians. There was no anti-Pol Pot leadership of national stature during the Pol Pot years—no de Gaulle or Ho Chi Minh who, by their resistance from abroad and by their appeal to their compatriots to take up arms, earned a legitimacy during their country's occupation that allowed them to lead it subsequently. There was opposition, of course, but it was private, however widespread. On the Left, the most outstanding and long-standing opponent of Pol Pot, and certainly a charismatic figure in his own right, Hou Yuon, was the first to be killed, in 1975. Later, it seems from the evidence at Tuol Sleng, the main prison and torture centre for Pol Pot detainees, a network of resistance was established, which included famous Cambodian leftists like Hu Nim, Tiv Ol, Phouk Chhay. All were arrested, tortured, broken and killed. A section of the socialist resistance escaped to Vietnam, some even before 1975. But Hanoi's policy was to try to prevent an open breach with the Phnom Penh regime, and none on its soil was allowed openly to attack Pol Pot, until after the latter broke off relations with Vietnam at the end of 1977.

On the Right, none of Pol Pot's capitalist opponents died in the fight against him, unlike so many on the Left. Yet not one raised the flag of resistance unequivocally when there was a chance to do so. In a speech in December 1979, Hun Sen, Cambodia's 29 year-old Foreign Minister, asked why the various right-ists who rushed to the Thai border from France after the Vietnamese had over-thrown Pol Pot had not gone there before. It is an apt question. By 1977 it was evident that Pol Pot's regime was unpopular and unstable, purging its cadres and becoming increasingly bellicose. Despite all the denunciations of 'human rights violations', no call to arms was made or allowed, by Khmer in Europe or America. In effect, Hun Sen charges that Washington knew—as it certainly did—of Pol Pot's hostility to Vietnam and wished to do nothing to deflect it; hence its refusal to fund a rightist opposition.

Nor can Sihanouk propose himself as a principled opponent of Pol Pot's rule. He returned to Cambodia, and palace arrest, knowing the situation, and he defended Pol Pot at the United Nations when he had his one great chance to strike out from an independent position, with the Vietnamese still keeping their options open in his respect. All parties might welcome the legitimacy Sihanouk would bestow, but none wishes to see him regain political power. And he seems to have forfeited his claim to such power by his equivocation with regard to Pol Pot.

Just as history cannot be rolled back to 1970, to undo the Lon Nol coup, so an historic opposition to Pol Pot by a national hero cannot now be created retrospec-tively. No such leader emerged and lived. This is a fact of grave psychological proportions for Cambodians in their struggle for self-liberation from their own past. It is little wonder that passivity and fatalism seem widespread. When the capital was liberated last year, a song was composed which I have heard draw a real response from the new establishment. Called after the city, it is a lament in traditional style. Roughly translated, its main refrain: 'Phnom Penh, Phnom Penh, for three years I have thought of you in sorrow, Phnom Penh.'

Khmer fatalism compounds the threat to the Vietnamese of Sino-American pressure along the Thai border. They are relied upon as the only security against a Pol Pot return, yet suspected of harbouring no desire to leave. How can a socialist state be created in such circumstances, even if it is only in the most elementary stage of economic development? Many fear the imposition of rigid social and economic controls. With liberalisation the order of the day in Vietnam this seems unlikely. But Pol Pot himself claimed to be socialist, which does not help the new regime at all. There is also a problem of 'style'—which I believe signals a crisis for Vietnamese communism. Getting into Cambodia today from the West is difficult, and will remain so until the regime is recognised. But once there, government officials are easier to see and more relaxed and helpful than they are in Hanoi, where bureaucracy and division of information baffles even old hands. Cambodia is a land of hammocks, of gossip transformed into hyperbole over late-night fires,

Pol Pot and after: regimental meetings give way to a more informal style after the end of the regime—above: 1978; below: 1981.

of easy deals. The Vietnamese style of argued consensus, of public secrecy, of self-possession, is remarkably different. But what counts today is not so much the contrast in 'national character' as the difference in the specific experience and circumstances of the two national leaderships. The world which formed the senior members of the Vietnamese administration is not the world which has been experienced by the younger men now trying to run Cambodia.

There is also a manifest difference of 'position' in the world between Phnom Penh and Hanoi. The former is much closer to the West. Daily flights touch down from Bangkok. Hanoi is quite out of touch, by comparison. There is the absolute difference in experience of revolution. The secrecy, the patience, the deviousness and the caution which Ho developed demonstrated an accurate appreciation of Vietnamese realities, and served well against the United States. The secrecy, obedience and control created by Pol Pot had quite other qualities.

Any attempt to impose a Hanoi style on Phnom Penh's new cadres would have little chance of working. Thus the Vietnamese themselves will have to change, or fail. There are signs that they might change. A year ago the official Hanoi line was that Vietnamese troops entered Cambodia only after a massive Heng Samrin-led uprising. In November 1979, at the UN, this interpretation was followed by a plea that Vietnam acted in self-defence. In Le Duc Tho's December 1979 statement an historically realistic order of events is made. The importance of this shift is that it involves a certain abandonment of propaganda for frankness. And if there is to be a Cambodian 'self-liberation' then Cambodian socialists must be able to speak frankly to the Vietnamese in public—not least because the Vietnamese themselves have been implicated by the rise of Pol Pot. Their responsibility may be a fraction of that borne by the United States and China; nonetheless it exists. The point may seem to be one for historians, but in fact it could be critical for the development of relations between Vietnam and Cambodia today. Vietnamese officials will say that 'Pol Pot deceived us', but how was this possible? If the new leaders of Cambodia are eventually to stand before their people (and their own cadres) with self-assurance, they cannot project a version of the events which brought them to power, in which the role of Vietnam was entirely far-sighted and disinterested.

What future lies before Cambodia? In the short-run everything turns on getting the rice seeds in for the harvest at this year's end. In the longer run a nationalist explosion cannot be ruled out. But it seems unlikely that a popular insurgency will develop from the protracted warfare the Chinese are now fuelling by supporting Pol Pot in his Thai sanctuaries. Everyone seems to agree that the majority of Khmers prefer the presence of the Vietnamese with their *laissez-faire* policy, to Pol Pot's return and the threat of more terror.

The allegiance of the Cambodian army will be critical in determining the future state machine in Phnom Penh. A poor and oppressive dictatorship is one possibility, which will become a permanent burden upon its conqueror. As I left from Phnom Penh's Potchenchong airport, Husak's portrait was on display next to Heng Samrin's, in preparation for a state visit from the Czechs; an ominous symbol of such an eventuality. But if there is one rule about Cambodia that has yet to be broken, it is that all predictions made about its destiny are proved wrong. Perhaps it is fortunate, then, that no one has predicted the emergence of a relaxed and healed country, in the course of the next decade. This year, everything depends on getting the aid through and the rice planted.

(28 March 1980)

Only the allies are new
John Pilger

A few miles from Cambodia, on the Thailand border, is a surburban Fort Apache now sluiced with red mud as the monsoon settles over Indochina. It is a warren of attractive houses on piles, accommodating newly prosperous Thai families whose pick-up trucks and polythene-wrapped Hondas, and tape decks and winsome children, reflect the entrepreneurial opportunities of the past year, delivered by the unique tragedy across the border. There is a supermarket, proclaiming 'Pepsi Superman' and 'For Rent' signs ('Short or Long Time'; the ambiguity, strictly Thai, embraces a wide range of leasing); and there are foreigners, with pensions secure and motives not entirely altruistic, for which these services are intended.

The Catholic Relief Services has a house here, a place of urgency commanded by a former Green Berets officer, now a Jesuit priest. A short distance away is the border headquarters of UNICEF, the United Nations Children's Fund, with its hi-there receptionist, Year of the Child decor and refrigerated air conditioning; and there is the World Relief 'post', from which thirteen missionaries of the Assembly of God go forth into the Khmer Rouge fortress of Sa Kaeo, known locally as a United Nations refugee camp, to inform thousands of opaque eyes that Jesus Christ will save them, if not their victims. In 1979 Rosalynn Carter came to the same camp and said America would save them, which was more to the point.

This is Aranyaprathet, Thailand, overlaid with Amarillo, Texas and Saigon before it 'fell'—the latter familiar to, and mourned by, many of the foreigners here. Indeed, outside Prol's restaurant, where *everybody* goes, the Hondarised cowboys wear shades and black hats, evocative of the view from the verandah of the Continental Palace before it lapsed into communist hands; inside, with Simon and Garfunkel and other memories on tape, with hamburgers, Tom Collins and dry martinis served by children, the cowboys compromise an assortment of freelancers, some not unlike the *paparazzi* to which Michael Herr's 'Dispatches' was devoted, some on research grants, acknowledged 'experts' on a Cambodia they have not seen, some in the surgical uniforms of M*A*S*H with stethoscopes positioned for maximum chic, and which they appear reluctant to take off. Overhead: 'There's this Italian medical team sitting in Bangkok, right? We're up to here in fucking medical teams, but these guys are demanding a spot in the chorus line. Maybe they can take over the Valium programme. Three thousand

Eric Piper/Syndication International

Lionel Rosenblatt, head of KEG (Kampuchean Emergency Group), a branch of the US Embassy in Thailand which 'monitors' (i.e. manipulates) Western relief.

downers a day to the Pol Potters should keep them busy'. And there are tourists, asking: 'Does this place have a bathroom?' And there are men on United States Government business.

These men live in and work from a large house with a radio transmitter on the roof and a fleet of unmarked white station wagons coming and going and which also have transmitters. This is the operations base of the Kampuchea Emergency Group, or KEG, whose activities somehow have escaped the otherwise saturation media coverage of the humanitarian aspects of the border. The men of KEG are attached to the US Embassy in Bangkok and report variously to the State Department, USAID, the CIA and, of course, to Ambassador Morton Abramowitz, a Pentagon China specialist who two years ago replaced Charles Whitehouse, an advocate of 'normalising' with Vietnam, and whose appointment was greeted by a Bangkok newspaper with these comments:

> As his past activities indicate, Abramowitz is one hope of the United States in its effort to cooperate with China to block Soviet and Vietnamese influence in South East Asia.

Both the appointment of Abramowitz and the setting up of KEG were the decisions of Dr Zbigniew Brzezinski, President Carter's National Security Adviser who, it might be fairly said, has taken over where Dr Henry Kissinger left off, as the West's leading warlord. Certainly, the current American war in Indochina, in which American blood, B52s and the products of the Dow Chemical Company are not needed, is his.

Enter Lionel A. Rosenblatt, formerly of the United States Embassy, Saigon, now 'refugee co-ordinator' of KEG, Thailand, whose words are these:

> I feel that what we're doing is an appropriate extension of our war in Vietnam. I think it's important for America to remember its *responsibilities* in this region,

even though it doesn't have the high security threshhold that we used to have with half a million men here. I think that actually the only problem with America in this part of the world is that, having fought the Vietnam war, most people at home have retired completely in terms of involvement. Well, the people who are working here with us, some are old Indochina hands and some aren't, are people who are interested in seeing that humanitarian effort continue, who are concerned about the life-threatening processes here. Okay, so the general inclination is forget South East Asia, that was the sixties, early seventies. Now *we* say we need to be involved, and there *will* be an increasing US involvement in South East Asia in the 1980s. And the new line, if you like, is right here in Thailand, okay?

Deja vu! With the exception of Life Threatening Processes (LTP?), which is new issue, such words might have come echoing through that fabled, unlit tunnel of the sixties and seventies, had they not been uttered the other day, though I have to say that to describe the Vietnam war as a 'humanitarian effort' is premature; history is being re-written in South East Asia, but not *that* quickly. The mission of KEG is indeed the 'appropriate extension': it is to oversee the distribution of Western supplies, which are funded largely by the United States and the EEC, including Britain, to the proxies in the latest Indochina war: the 'guerrilla forces' with a haven on the border, namely the Khmer Rouge, proportionately the most thorough mass murderers in modern times, whose demonry included the building of Auschwitz in Asia*, whom even the President of the United States has described as 'the world's worst violaters of human rights'.

This strategy is being carried out under the cover of humanitarianism; its objective is, to borrow from Dr Kissinger, the 'destabilisation' of Cambodia and, more important, of Vietnam. The following effects are desired: the isolation and wrecking of Vietnam's economy, so that its spirit is finally broken and its revolution converted to the brutalised, authoritarian image into which it is presently cast, thereby forcing it into satellite dependency on the Soviet Union; the discrediting, in the eyes of the world, of a generation of Vietnamese struggle and sacrifice, so that the US intervention in Indochina and its use of Vietnam as a laboratory of rampant war technology is historically justified, thereby legitimising future adventures and drawing revenge for the humiliation of a 'lost' war; and the continuation of an unwanted war of attrition between the Soviet Union and China and of the obsession of each with the other's 'expansionism' (Mao's original revisionist charge having faded into obsolescence now that the 'Sound of Music' is ensconced in Peking). This is the Brzezinski strategy for the 1980s. There is no reason to doubt that it will be the Reagan strategy. Divide and rule, I believe it is called.

Brzezinski's Indochina war began with Ambassador Abramowitz's arrival in Bangkok in the summer of 1978 and the subsequent abandonment of a momentous chance of peace, to which reference should be made here because it went largely unreported and because it offers a perspective on Vietnam's relationship with the Soviet Union that is very different from the currently propagated version. In the autumn of 1978 a mission of doctors and nutritionists sent by Senator Edward Kennedy's Committee on Vietnam reported 'shock' at the health of the Vietnamese people they saw and appealed to President Carter to 'bring the people of Vietnam back from the precipice of calamity... and to save thousands of men,

---

* See Part IV: The bureaucracy of death.

women and children by a single act of magnanimity'. The report made special mention of extreme food shortages and the need of skimmed milk for children. On the advice of Dr Brzezinski, the President's response was to sign a renewal of the total American embargo of Vietnam, including food.

It was then that Vietnam's overtures to America, of which little was heard in the West and which the Vietnamese saw as the means of extricating themselves from the cold war between the Soviet Union and China, became exhausted. An abbreviation of an excellent analysis by Derek Davies, editor of the conservative *Far Eastern Economic Review*, is worth quoting here:

> At the time of Carter's election at the end of 1976 Moscow was losing ground in Vietnam... Vietnamese Vice-Foreign Minister Phan Hien had made it clear that Vietnam did not accept the view of ASEAN (Association of South East Asian Nations) as an imperialist creation, nor did it support the Soviet proposal for an Asian collective security treaty. At home, Vietnam was re-absorbing the South with kid gloves.
>
> Hanoi had irritated Moscow with its membership of the World Bank, the IMF and the Asian Development Bank and was bent on improving relations with China. Peking was responding, recalling the late premier Chou En Lai's concern for Vietnam. In the spring of 1977, Hanoi publicly confirmed the pragmatism with which it was prepared to tackle its economic problems. It promulgated a foreign investment code which was both liberal and flexible, providing for joint enterprises and wholly-owned foreign projects. In the spring of 1978 Pham Van Dong indicated that Vietnam would be willing to drop all preconditions to talks with the Americans—even reparations. There was no response from Washington. The US again voted against the (Asian Development) bank being used to channel funds to Vietnam.

'The tragic circle', as Davies describes the American rebuff, was closed when Vietnam had no alternative but to slip further into the Soviet sphere. (Indeed, I am reliably told, two officials of the Asian Development Bank were instructed to 'lose the files on Vietnam'.)

With famine a real prospect, there also was no alternative but to end the 'Cholon Chinese' control of the rice market in southern Vietnam, and this helped to precipitate the first substantial and brutally encouraged exodus of 'boat people'. With Chinese military advisers at his elbow, Pol Pot increased his attacks on the ricelands of the 'Parrot's Beak' to a level of almost daily atrocities in Vietnamese border villages; and finally the Vietnamese, who had offered the Khmer Rouge a demilitarised border with international inspection, had little choice but to 'invade' Pol Pot's charnel house (Why is it that we think of Europe as having been 'liberated', not 'invaded'?) and, in so doing, put an end to the genocide of the Khmer people. Vietnam, having journeyed through a history of courage and pain, with millions dead and maimed, and having expelled both its colonial masters and a great power (which no other small country has ever done) was now an international pariah; and with the nod from Washington—that is from Brzezinski, *not* from Cyrus Vance—China attacked massively from the north.

In July 1980, in Tokyo, President Carter and Chairman Hua Guofeng met for the first time. It was indeed 'an historic meeting', as their spokesmen effused; for here was the remarkable alliance begun by Nixon and Kissinger in 1972 being consummated with the tacit agreement that the Pentagon would arm China (no longer, 'Red China', of course) and with the following communiqué:

> There is essential agreement between the United States and the People's Republic of China with regard to strategic perspectives and particularly as they relate to... the invasion of Cambodia by Soviet-backed Vietnamese.

In other words, it would seem that America has abandoned the relatively cautious position taken by Secretary Vance before his resignation—that Washington neither supported the Phnom Penh government nor the Khmer Rouge—and has given full approval to China's Indochina policy, which is to subdue Vietnam, by force or attrition, and to restore the Khmer Rouge to power in 'Democratic Kampuchea' with a new, respectable image and, should America insist, in the

Eric Piper/Syndication International

Jack Williamson, US 'Co-ordinator' with the Thai army on the Thai border.

guise of a 'non-aligned' coalition. The United States and its Western partners already are playing their part by supplying the 'new' Khmer Rouge with 'relief'.

This returns us to the Thai border, where the new line is drawn, and to those who implement the American side of the bargain, or 'the increasing involvement in the 1980s', as the Deer Hunters of the Kampuchean Emergency Group see it. Indeed, the identity of the chief of KEG underscores the unflagging continuity of American involvement in Indochina. He is Colonel Michael Eiland, an illustrious Deer Hunter. In 1969/70 Eiland, then a major, was operations officer of a clandestine Special Forces group code-named Daniel Boone which, as William Shawcross documents in *Sideshow: Kissinger, Nixon and the Destruction of Cambodia**, was responsible for the reconnaissance of the secret and illegal bombing

---

* André Deutsch, 1979.

that tore apart Cambodia's fragile neutrality and ushered in a decade of war and butchery and, as a consequence, was a catalyst for the triumph of the Khmer Rouge. Colonel Eiland, having indirectly given the Khmer Rouge a helping hand a decade ago, is once again reaching out to them, though several million people have died in the interim.

In seniority, a commanding, burly figure in a yellow baseball cap is above both Rosenblatt and Eiland. He is Jack Williamson, who was the USAID man in Laos during the 'destabilising' there in the early seventies. He is now the Pentagon's most important man in Thailand. 'Williamson's job', I was told, 'is to see that the Thais don't lose their nerve or focus on what's important: support for anti-Vietnamese forces, and that means Pol Pot'.

Williamson 'co-ordinates' and 'advises' Task Force 80, a special Thai Army intelligence unit assigned to 'police' the border camps. What that means is that Thai officers in civilian clothes command guerrilla groups both inside Thailand and when they move back into Cambodia. When a *Philadelphia Inquirer* reporter discovered 'Camp 42', a Khmer base run entirely by Thais, he was imprisoned and his film destroyed. Task Force 80 draws most of its funding *direct* from the US Embassy in Bangkok.

In the past few weeks the facade of the humanitarian operation along the border has begun to crumble. This is not to suggest that the international and voluntary relief agencies did not save a great many lives last year, when people fled from the Khmer Rouge enclaves in search of food, nor is it to impugn the motives of many individual aid officials. Indeed, it is the most dedicated among the aid people who now talk openly and with rising bitterness of their manipulation by their own bureaucracies, by the Thai military and by the Americans in Bangkok and on the border.

One UNICEF official was recalled to New York and threatened with dismissal if he continued to speak publicly of this manipulation and especially of Vietnam's humanitarian assistance to Cambodia, evidence of which he had seen. For agency people like him, the repatriation of 8,600 from the Thai camps is the sorest case in point. All these 'returnees' came from Sa Kaeo camp, inside Thailand, which the United Nations High Commission for Refugees (UNHCR) administers, nominally, and the Khmer Rouge control in reality, dispensing aid and intimidation, not to mention burying people up to their necks as sport.

The Khmer Rouge in this camp have been rested and fattened by Western aid and, said a UN official who watched the first batch leave, 'they're ready to fight… we're sending back an entire division of the bastards. This is like a declaration of war'. An official of CARE, the American relief organisation, said, 'In a few months we'll have the starving babies back on television, the products of a war which this repatriation stunt makes damn sure will go on, and on.' The *Bangkok Post* reported:

The followers of toppled premier Pol Pot, who exercises a strong hold over many of the camp's 30,000 refugees, want as many to return as possible to help wage a guerrilla war against Vietnam's forces. Pol Pot officials have been telling refugees that the United Nations would cut off food aid to them if they refused repatriation and that they had to return to Pol Pot controlled areas of the Thai-Kampuchean border. The Pol Pot followers, some of whom have told interviewers that they took part in mass executions during Pol Pot's days in power, have a ditty to reinforce their point. It goes:

Those of you who go back first will sleep on cots,
Those who go back second will sleep on mats,
Those who go back third will sleep in mud,
Those who go back last will sleep under the ground.

The UNHCR Chief Coordinator, Zia Rizvi, attempted to postpone the repatriation, but was turned down by the Thais. Predictably, the Vietnamese responded to the provocation with an attack that closed the 'land bridge' at Nong Chan and has stopped, perhaps only temporarily, the agencies' regular supply runs to such Khmer Rouge bases as Phnom Malai and Ta Prik in the south and Phnom Chat in the north. Certainly, my own journey across the border, to Phnom Chat, produced a spectacle of proof of how UNICEF and the Red Cross have restored the Khmer Rouge and helped to mould them into an effective force now estimated at 30,000 troops, or *double* their strength since the inception of 'cross border feeding'.

I travelled in a UNICEF Land Rover at the head of a convoy of forty trucks: seventeen loaded with food, seventeen with seed and the rest with agricultural kits and assorted 'goodies', which is a quaint term the agency people use for the West's largesse. Phnom Chat is a Khmer Rouge operations base set in forest, and bunkered, with land mines every fifteen yards. These were laid by courtesy of the Thai army, which keeps a commando unit encamped (and not very well camouflaged) on the periphery of the base *inside* Cambodia.

The base itself has a Task Force 80 'liaison officer' who was worried and displeased by the presence of foreigners other than those bearing 'goodies'. The UNICEF official leading the convoy, Phyllis Gestrin, a University of Texas psychology professor, was also worried and clearly disliked what she was doing. 'I don't want to think what this aid is doing: I don't trust these blackshirts,' she said.

Indeed, she could barely suppress her fear and turned the Land Rover around and pointed it back along the track. 'I always do this,' she said, 'so I can make a quick getaway'. Later, in a state of mounting unease, Phyllis drove us into a tree, then over ground which she earlier had pointed out as a possible minefield. 'Oh man', she said, 'this place gives me the creeps. Let's get it over with'.

When the forty trucks had dumped their 'goodies' at sheds in a clearing, Phyllis solicited the signature of one of three Khmer Rouge who had watched in silence from a thatched shelter, like the framed silhouettes of hanged men. 'I guess what I got here is a receipt', said Phyllis, attempting a little laugh.

As we were preparing to leave, UNICEF's chief of North West Operations in Thailand, Ulf Krisstoffersson, arrived and proceeded to explain to me a complicated monitoring system that entailed checking 'non-resident family groups'. 'But', I said, 'the trucks have dumped the loads at the feet of the Khmer Rouge and it's they who distribute it'. 'Well, yes,' he said, 'but I want you to understand it gets to civilians, too. Many of these people are not Khmer Rouge; they're Khmer Serei'.

The Khmer Serei are usually described as 'right wing guerrillas'; in fact, their leaders are bandits who, with the Thais, run the black market and gold trade in the refugee camps on the Thai side. They have no real popular following; and what the Thai military is doing is grafting civilians, with no particular allegiance, on to Khmer Rouge bases—so that they can proceed with the fiction that the Khmer Rouge and the Khmer Serei are united against the Vietnamese. This also creates a

Eric Piper/Syndication International

Khmer Rouge receiving the West's largesse—some of the 40 truck loads of supplies delivered to a base inside Cambodia at Phnom Chat.

justification for humanitarian aid, although the beneficiaries of the aid are clearly *not* civilians, who look undernourished as well as terrified. By contrast, the Khmer Rouge are well fed and muscled. 'Okay', said Krisstoffersson, 'that man over there is a butcher and we're feeding his army, but *we* are not political.'

The 'butcher' is the base commander, a senior Pol Pot man who likes the foreign aid people to call him 'Monsieur Le President'. I asked to see Monsieur Le President and was assured that he would 'appear'; and I was soon confronted by a man with the calcified face of a small boy, and static eyes.

In 1979, in Siem Reap province, I saw the mass grave of several thousand people, many of whom had been beaten to death. Now, smiling before me, was Pol Pot's equivalent of the governor of that province. His name is Nam Phann, which is probably a military alias. He was eager to confirm that Western aid had indeed sustained and restored the Khmer Rouge '... and thank you very much, and we wish for more'.

He said that 'our friends in the world' were the United Nations, the countries of ASEAN, especially Thailand and Singapore, and the United States. 'Oh yes, the United States!', he said, with feeling. But what of all the stories of atrocities and genocide under Pol Pot? 'Oh *that*', he replied. 'Those stories are completely untrue. They were made up by the Vietnamese to confuse the world.'

The agencies cannot plead naiveté; Red Cross medical teams have ministered to the Khmer Rouge inside Cambodia, at Ta Prik and Nong Pou, knowing that these are logistical forward positions. Our request to accompany them was refused; not even the day of departure could be disclosed. Why should a strictly humanitarian mission be secret?

'You must not be too hard on us', said a Red Cross official. 'The whole thing is rotten and we're sitting here in the middle of the garbage, trying to get off. What are we to do when Task Force 80 brings Khmer Rouge wounded to Sa Kaeo camp (inside Thailand) in the middle of the night and orders our teams to treat them? Of course, we have to patch them up, and the Thais send them back. If we pull out of the border, the Thais will prevent our supplies going through Bangkok to Phnom Penh, and the Phnom Penh authorities will regard us as accessories to their enemy, and make life difficult for our people there. It's an impossible situation for us.'

A senior UNICEF man said, 'I have the US embassy and the KEG people on the phone every day now. They keep telling us to hang in there. Well, I am fed up, and I want to get out. But they know that *we* know that if we desert the border, US funds will dry up. It's the crudest form of manipulation.'

Both the international agencies and the Americans have canvassed the voluntary agencies for those willing to take over the supply runs to the Khmer Rouge. Even the Catholic Relief Services, which always has had close relations with the Americans, has refused to 'hang in there'.

'They'll find some Volag (voluntary agency) to do it', said a former UN official. 'Most of them are Christian and anti-Communist and some are no more than cowboys, with too much money and too little to do, and feeding Pol Pot or flying out a jumbo load of lactating mothers is all the same to them'.

In July 1980 James Grant, the new executive director of UNICEF, said in London:

> Reports that relief supplies are to be cut off in two weeks time are unfounded. The aim is to continue the supply of relief in situations where assurance can be given *by the Thai Government* that the aid is going only to civilian groups and not to Khmer guerrilla forces.

The italics are mine; the gall is his. The problem for Mr Grant, for UNICEF and for the Red Cross is that these Western government-funded agencies are now seen to be doing *precisely* what the Phnom Penh authorities have accused them of doing. Readers may recall last year's orchestrated public outcry, mostly from Geneva and New York, that the Phnom Penh government would not allow the agencies to send in a monitoring force of some 50 officials. There are now 78 aid officials in Phnom Penh; and whatever the shortcomings of effective relief monitoring *inside* Cambodia (Kampuchea), there is virtually none across the Thai border, which has received a hugely disproportionate share of Western charity.

Indeed, an internal UNICEF estimate is that 84 per cent of rice sent across the border is sold. By attracting up to 20 per cent of the population toward the border, farmers and draft animals are drawn away from the fields and from planting seed for the vital December harvest, the success of which will determine whether or not the nation is able to feed itself or is to remain dependent on foreign welfare. I have met few aid officials who do not regard the magnet of the border as an indirect means of de-stabilisation.

Aside from shoring up the Khmer Rouge, there are other direct methods. Before I went to the Thai border I travelled extensively in Cambodia, including up to within a few miles of the border. A farmer, Ses Kravah, who has worked his fields in the village of Kob for thirty years, lamented that his crop would be stunted and a disastrous harvest assured. He had received seed from Phnom Penh, but had decided to buy most of his seed from across the nearby border, only to discover bags of empty husks and a germination rate of less than forty per cent. The World Food Programme has dumped, from the Thai side of the border, a great deal of

this low-grade seed, for which the invoices can be traced to the US Embassy in Bangkok.

The distortion in the West of events in Indochina, which have allowed Washington to play its 'China Card' and Western governments (and the relief agencies) to cast themselves as saviours and the Vietnamese and the Phnom Penh government as wicked and obstructionist, has effectively complemented the de-stabilising activities along the border, where the media coverage has concentrated. (So much so that children in Kao I Dung camp have produced a piece of melancholy theatre that tells the story of Cambodia's suffering, beginning with little soliloquies about murder and starvation and ending with a tableau of foreign television crews gaping emptily at the dead.)

It is now clear that the insidious propaganda against Cambodia has been planned. In the *Guardian* of 8 January 1980 John Gittings reported.

> The Brzezinski strategy of crudely dividing Peking from Hanoi (thus pushing the Vietnamese toward Moscow) is compounded of deep feelings of hostility toward the only Asians who have managed to defeat the United States in war. One adviser on his staff has recently called Vietnam a 'cesspool of humanity.' Last November, State Department sources revealed their intention of mounting an international propaganda offensive to spread atrocity stories about Vietnamese behaviour in Kampuchea. Within days, presumably on White House instructions, US journalists in Bangkok and Singapore were shown the appropriate 'refugee stories' and Dr Brzezinski himself verbally briefed a distinguished foreign correspondent Washington columnist over lunch on the contents of 'the latest CIA report.'

Stories began to appear in the American press that this 'latest CIA report' charged that the Vietnamese were burning crops, laying mines in paddies, stealing food, even preventing planting and that the Soviet Union also was blocking food distribution. Editorialists trumpeted 'genocide', and liberal columnists atoned for their sins during the war and Watergate and printed, at times verbatim, that which Brzezinski's office fed them. It was as if the clock had spun back twenty years, and the Pentagon Papers had never happened. Of course, the CIA report was a fabrication. Indeed, it was not a report at all; it was warmed-over propaganda that rejected a genuine CIA analysis, whose author recently told a Washington-based Indochina research group, 'They misrepresented everything I wrote.'

Shortly after the 'report' was given to the press, I was asked by a Western foreign minister to give my observations of what I had seen in Cambodia. I told him that the only substantial relief my ATV team and I had seen was that coming from Vietnam, that we had followed a civilian convoy coming over the 'land bridge' from Saigon to its recipients among the Khmer population, that the only doctors we had seen were Vietnamese and that every Khmer we had spoken to spoke the obvious truth: that the Vietnamese had saved their lives.

'Yes, I know that', he said. 'But', I asked, 'Haven't you seen the CIA report?' 'Yes', he replied 'the State Department told us to ignore it, that it was only for the media.'

The 'diversion of aid', and 'Vietnamese atrocity' stories have been discredited by every journalist who has been to Cambodia, including those hostile to Vietnam, and by all relief officials. Dominic Dufour, chief of the Red Cross mission in Phnom Penh, told me, 'Apart from minor pilfering, the stories of misuse have come from outside as propaganda and are rubbish. Why should the

Vietnamese give with one hand and take with the other?' Even Ambassador Abramowitz has been moved to say there was no proof that the Vietnamese were committing 'subtle genocide'. As for the Russians blocking aid, the State Department's current assessment shows the Soviet Union as the biggest single donor. But the momentum, or 'drip effect', of this type of propaganda, familiar to most foreign correspondents (and documented in a fine article by Philip Jacobson in the *Sunday Times,* July 1980, had left its stain.

On 28 December 1979 Alistair Cooke, in his BBC *Letter from America,* spoke of 'a document that has been delivered into the hands of the President of the United States and one that made him *furious'.* Speaking of The President and The Document (the bogus CIA report) in his customary hallowed tones, Cooke accused the Vietnamese and the Russians of plotting to block 'great supplies and medicines that could save unaccountable lives in Cambodia.'

I mention Cooke's broadcast because it was delivered during the Christmas period when a great many people in this country were deeply concerned about Cambodia. Tens of thousands had given to Oxfam and other agencies; and many of them were those who could least afford to give. Every day for several months they had sent family allowances, life savings, holiday money, dole money and pocket money; the rescue of Cambodia had become something of a national cause in Britain, above and in spite of politics, especially among children; the Blue Peter appeal raised £3,500,000. No doubt some of these people heard Cooke's broadcast, and the lie he repeated would have dismayed them. He was one of many who did that. Never have I known so many pundits tending the same little garden of bigotry; Cambodia's suffering seemed to draw them out. That no reporter who went to Cambodia confirmed such pernicious rubbish says something about the nature of journalism.

I went back to Cambodia in July 1980, accompanied by Jim Howard, who started Oxfam's operation, and two French doctors who were the only Western doctors in Cambodia when I was there in 1979. I had asked them to return with me, believing that only those who had seen Cambodia's landscape of famine then could make a fair assessment now.

So great are the problems remaining in a society whose very fabric has unravelled, with no family I met grieving the death of fewer than six members, that the task of restoration would daunt the most advanced nation; and this is a peasant society, with its educated and skilled decimated. For example, last year the Ministry of Health consisted of a Minister, a deputy and an old Renault car with a flat battery and no tyres. Today this ministry, which has just five senior officials working from what was the old Volkswagen showrooms, is much criticised by foreign officials for its 'lack of efficiency'. Last August the hospital at Kompong Speu, which comes under the Ministry of Health, had no drugs, no bandages, no beds, no blankets. It was not a hospital at all; the Khmer Rouge, in their orgy of demolition and vandalism, had *erased* it in the almost ingenious way they had dismantled the Roman Catholic Cathedral in Phnom Penh, leaving not a stone.

After Battambang province, Kompong Speu was probably the most wasted, plundered and brutalised area of Cambodia. In August 1979, a lone Vietnamese doctor insisted on splashing Dettol on us; for there was cholera, plague and anthrax. Dr Jean-Michel Vinot, one of the French doctors who accompanied me, said:

I remember a whole ward of orphans died in one week; there was *nothing.* Now they have a functioning hospital, and a dispensary with a whole range of drugs. The most serious case I can find is a child with meningitis, and she will survive.

When we were last here, Dr Vinot estimated that eighty per cent of the women in Kompong Speu had lost their menstrual cycle, as a direct result of the trauma of life under a regime which—in forging together the outer reaches of Maoism with a barbaric and glorified medievalism—outlawed not only the family, but all sentiment and expressions of love and grief. Today the hospital has an overflowing maternity ward. 'The transformation and resilience', said Dr Vinot, 'is *incredible*'.

Ian Hopwood of UNICEF has calculated that 912,000 children are now in schools throughout Cambodia. 'Many of the 19,000 teachers have never taught before', he said, 'but the Government has introduced a two-month crash course and it appears to be working'. In August 1979, in Phnom Penh, Jim Howard found fifty sick and starving children in what had been converted to a pig pen. In ten months this place has been transformed into the largest primary school in the country, with desks, paper, pencils, toys, footballs: most of them paid for in Britain. In the playground, as in the pavement outside, as in towns all over the country, are palm trees planted by the Khmer Rouge, beneath which has been discovered human fertiliser. Here, the children, now in hot pursuit of a cheated childhood, use them as goalposts.

When we arrived in Phnom Penh in 1979, the city stood virtually as it had been abandoned, with rubbish tips inhabited by little phantoms, mostly orphaned children, attempting to use worthless banknotes as fuel and to eat a gruel of roots and plants. I remember the presence of death, not of rotting corpses, but of something surreal and pervasive in the humidity and stillness; this had been a city whose population had swollen to more than two million and all of them had been

Eric Piper/Syndication International

Football in the playground—each young palm tree planted by Pol Pot was fertilised by a body; the football comes from Britain.

marched, at gunpoint, into the countryside and perhaps half of them are now dead.

Today, Phnom Penh has more than 100,000 people, traffic, shops, restaurants, weddings, two raucous markets, electricity, water (the waterworks restored with British money) a textile factory, a drugs factory, reopened pagodas, telephones, two bus routes, a jazz band, a football team and currency; the successful introduction of the *riel*, in April and May 1980, as an achievement which all good monetarists surely must regard as remarkable.

Although we saw none of the starvation we saw last summer, which the Khmer now recall as 'the great months of death', we did see pockets of worrying malnutrition among children. In Battambang railway yards, very thin children swept rolling stock with their hands for rice seed. They have survived and they exude the kind of energy that seems resourceless, but I suspect it will take just one epidemic to decimate them. Bill Yates, Oxfam's chief in Phnom Penh, believes the Government has taken a gamble to stockpile and ration food, giving priority to seed distribution for the December harvest. He said:

> They have trusted in the peasants' natural instinct to live off the land, and everyone who needs to work and has no source of food, from nurses to bridge repairers, is receiving rations. All the villages I have seen have subsistence plots of maize corn, sugar cane and fruit, and I haven't seen a sow that isn't pregnant. I may be wrong, but I think the relief agencies may have been outguessed by the government?

Certainly, although food distribution is sporadic and dangerously uneven, the opposite is true of seed. Unannounced, we watched seed unloaded from the Oxfam consortium's twentieth barge in Phnom Penh, followed it to the railway yards, then drove 350 miles to Battambang to see it unloaded and trucked to warehouses. The next day an armada of ox carts, donkey traps and cycles delivered the entire consignment of 390 tons to villages. From barge to soil took just three days.

There are myriad frustrations, obdurate officials, 'political' interferences etc. etc; and so what, one might ask, is new? The government is not a monolithic 'regime', as it is often presented; it is a confusion of students, teachers and other surviving remnants of the old bourgeoisie, *anyone* with skills, over whom preside men who defected from the Khmer Rouge and who, after a spot of re-education in Hanoi, are now keeping their heads down. There are crash-course cadres whose bored audiences want nothing to do with *any* political evangelism; one lady emerged from a political lecture and remarked that the name of a 'Mr Marx Lenin' had come up, whoever he was. (For the Vietnamese, this is another irony for the album; the unique experience of their so-called clients bears no resemblance to their own, and by shoring up a re-emerging urban elite, as they must, they are inadvertently re-creating again the divisions that, with Kissinger's bombs, helped to spawn the Khmer Rouge.)

After travelling with us, Jim Howard estimated that more than ninety per cent of the Oxfam consortium's relief had got through to 'end users'. Howard is probably one of the most experienced and respected 'disasters firemen', having been through India, Bangladesh and Biafra, and unlike some of the aid people in Phnom Penh, encamped in the old Hotel Royale, an Asian Wuthering Heights with stuffed crocodiles in the foyer and an atmosphere given to monastic claustro-

phobia, Howard sees problems from the point of view of *people,* and not from a Messianic complex, or a career. He said:

I think it will be a pity if ordinary people in Britain, who supported a faraway nation with their hearts and their savings, do not realise how much they have contributed to the rescue of Cambodia.

You see, for some of us in the relief business, the old colonialist fervour dies hard. How can the natives *possibly* have a government which might, just might, know its own people best? Their attitude is that the West knows best. The truth is that real corruption here has been negligible. *None* of the supplies are on sale in the market. The problem, which Westerners have difficulty with, is sensitivity. This is a government whose murderous enemy is still recognised by the United Nations and which rightly feels itself cut off and isolated fighting for its life. In the circumstances, I believe they have done an historic job of recovery.

Fear, not hunger, is Cambodia's burden now. It is a fear that threads through every conversation, that haunts every other face in every crowd. 'Will Pol Pot come back?' I was asked, time and again. In spite of the years of bombs and the West's backdoor support for Pol Pot, there seems little of the xenophobia toward Westerners that one would expect in a small nation that has suffered so much foreign vandalism. Traditional Khmer antipathy toward the Vietnamese has been shelved for the duration, and there is no manifest 'hatred' of which much has been made by those on the border. Vietnamese soldiers stroll through the markets, unarmed; their discipline is respected; people inside Cambodia know that only they stand between them and another Khmer Rouge regime.

The Monorom Hotel, where I stayed in Phnom Penh, arranged a 'disco night' recently. The girls and the children sat on one side of the room, palais style, and the men on the other. It was a lot of fun, until a cassette of the much-loved singer, Sin Sisamouth, was played, and people walked to the curtains and wept. He had been taken to Battambang, forced to dig his own grave and to sing the Khmer Rouge anthem, which is all about blood and death. Then he was beaten to death.

There is a unique train that carries seed from Phnom Penh to the north-west. On the return journey, every other day, it is a human ant heap with between five and ten thousand passengers, slung in hammocks between the wheels, embracing the funnel, sardined in the driver's cabin. The station master, a sardonic man, who spoke to me his first English in five years (knowledge of a foreign language under Pol Pot meant death) explained that the train could not proceed right to the Phnom Penh central station 'because the driver is no good; he is learning, you see. He does not know when to put on the brake, and when it is raining cats and frogs he is even worse!'

Two days later the train was ambushed by the Khmer Rouge with rockets and automatic weapons; at least 150 people were killed. When I told a Khmer friend that this had happened, her face became a mask, as if her feelings were incubated. It is a common expression and tears are rare.

She had been a radical student at Phnom Penh university when the Khmer Rouge marched silently into the city. 'With my comrades I went into the street to welcome them', she said.

One year later they had killed my sister, who was pregnant, my six brothers, my mother, my father. Just before the liberation, I knew they were going to kill me, but I ran into the forest. On that morning two little boys were accused of

stealing pigswill and we were brought out to watch them hanged. They were six
or seven years old.

Readers may know of such horrors, and I am sorry to have to repeat them. But as
the second Indochina war is fuelled, with the most populous nation and the most
powerful nation supporting those who murdered many children, memories are
fading almost as quickly as the killers' image is being refurbished. Khieu
Samphan, who has replaced Pol Pot as 'Prime Minister' of 'Democratic Kampuchea', has received the international press at his bush headquarters, courtesy of
the Thai military. *The Times* man in Bangkok, Neil Kelly, found him to be 'a
youthful, sturdy man with a ready smile' who 'wished to clear away the past' and
said that 'his government's future policy was to work for freedom for the people to
choose a government of any ideology—Communist, capitalist or middle of the
road'. *Ad nauseum.*

Such 'objective' interviews with a man who was the theoretician most responsible for the crimes against his people are not yet common; but they are emerging,
as if what the Khmer Rouge did was a mere political 'problem', not the mammoth
Nazi-like perversion it was. Dr Brzezinski's 'background' people already are
passing the word that 'Democratic Kampuchea' will, of course, have to be part of a
coalition, with or without Prince Sihanouk who has rather disturbed this vision by
saying he wants nothing to do with the butchers of his people.

Britain's Foreign Office has followed dutifully along; the Minister of State,
Peter Blaker, who gives the impression of having almost no knowledge of South
East Asia, has said repeatedly that the Vietnamese are no better than the Khmer
Rouge and that their 'puppets' in Phnom Penh control no national territory. Last
year, the Foreign Office applied unsubtle pressure to voluntary relief agencies,
warning them of 'grave difficulties' if they went ahead and sent relief to the Phnom
Penh government; Oxfam, to its great credit, ignored this. The perfidous effect, if
not the purpose, of Britain's 'de-recognition' of Pol Pot in December 1979 has
been to quieten opposition to the policy of backdoor support for the Khmer
Rouge; in May 1980, the Foreign Office instructed Sir Henry Yellowless, the
British delegate to the World Health Assembly, to vote *in favour* of the credentials
of 'Democratic Kampuchea'.

Pol Pot's (or Khieu Samphan's) representative at the United Nations, who
occupies a luxurious suite in the Beekman Tower hotel, has said there is no doubt
that, with Washington's and Peking's backing, the General Assembly will vote in
September in favour of the legitimacy of his 'government'. So the pieces are fitting
together. China, having rejected a lunar new year peace, has moved three new
divisions to its border with Vietnam, now in its thirty-fifth year of siege, and
suffering. As Deer Hunter Rosenblatt would say, another 'humanitarian effort' is
well under way.

(1 August 1980)

Sabotage of the defeated
Anthony Barnett

In Cambodia today, villagers and Ministers alike say they face a critical situation. The main harvest is badly down. Food stocks will run out at the beginning of 1982, in some areas perhaps catastrophically, unless alleviated by aid. Yet for a visitor returning after 18 months, the impression is not one of impending disaster, despite the startling signs of simultaneous flood and drought. One can stand on rice land baked so hard that the cracks swallow the wispy green seedlings, and then look up to see water stretching to the horizon. The contrast would seem inconceivable anywhere but here, a land of intense contradictions, a country whose death was once so lamented in the West, which has nonetheless definitely come back to life. Had the restitution taken place under Western auspices, it would have been celebrated in every supplement and TV channel, above all in America. Instead, the Cambodian achievement is an embarrassment, especially discomforting for those like the Americans, who still extend support at the United Nations to Pol Pot.

If you heard a lorry in February 1980, it was a rare sound, and an important one: was it one of the new Oxfam trucks? Did it carry rice? If full, where was it heading? Today, the main boulevards of Phnom Penh are busy with traffic, mostly bikes and motor bikes, with pedicabs and ponies. There are traffic accidents and break-downs. One of the symbols of the Pol Pot regime became the heaps of cars, dumped on the wayside. Many of these carcasses can still be seen, luxuriant vegetation engulfing their rusting hulks, in a way that recalls the famous images of Angkor. When the French first sent back etchings and impressions of the mediae-val temple complex, one of the strongest was of the trees whose roots held the stones together and overwhelmed them: symbol of a fallen greatness now being relentlessly digested by 'nature'. The image was part political, giving the Khmer a representation of themselves as a fallen and now incapable race, one saved by the generosity of French civilisation. Some of the fury of Pol Pot's ideology stemmed from an attempt to refute the colonial lie. This year the roads of the Cambodian capital witness a much more convincing rebuttal of the racialist myth. Far from being incapable, the Khmer have salvaged a surprising number of the vehicles discarded by Pol Pot, and they now outnumber the Soviet Ladas and the Toyotas given to the state.

The old engines, the Russian petrol, the broken exhausts of motor bikes, the bustle of half a million people in Phnom Penh (300,000 legal residents, most with cards, and the rest transient or squatters) has created problems of an order quite other than mere survival. Coming down the Mekong in the late afternoon, against a magnificent sky lit by the early orange glow of sunset, I could distinguish Phnom Penh not only by the silhouette of the Royal Palace, but also by a distinct cloud of unmistakable pollution. Progress!

Aid lorries are a normal sight. We passed a convoy of Oxfam and Unicef trucks taking seed to Svay Rieng. In a small district town in another province, six lorries unloaded seeds. The country men hauled the sacks to store; the loads were noted and signed for by officials with charge sheets. The drivers were townsmen. They had dark glasses and smart pants; their cabins were decorated with fetishes and baubles, and they were in a hurry to return. It was a routine delivery.

Another aid routine was a different sign of organised society. I was having lunch with a friend in a Chinese noodle restaurant in Phnom Penh. Across the road two men dropped a sack from a lorry and refastened its green tarpaulin, then drove off. Within a few minutes, a couple of young women came up and tried to move the sack but it was too heavy for them and they dropped it, with laughter. Having finished my soup, I strolled across to look more closely as the women sat on the pavement beside their prize: a sack of Italian aid rice. Neat, and in broad daylight.

The stabilisation is relative: the towns still look shattered, despite the busy populace; the factories are broken; many in the countryside are wretchedly poor. And there are the Pol Pot troops. Their ability to strike at targets has increased over the past year, as they have been better equipped by China, under the eye of the United States in Thailand. But although they are more effective in strike power, there are no signs that the Khmer Rouge have won any political support; on the contrary the feeling of security is significantly greater. Eighteen months ago, people were still uncertain: would there be another war, would their reprieve from Pol Pot be merely temporary? Today, despite successful raids, the Khmer Rouge forces favoured by the UN have been reduced to terrorists.

The cost remains high. The train to Battambang was derailed in August 1981, and rumour has it that 20 or so were killed before the Pol Pot assailants fled. It was at least the third such attack. Yet there were still passengers waiting at the station to go West. There was a successful ambush that month against the head of Prey Veng province, whose vehicle was mined, apparently by some dismissed subordinates, one of whom escaped arrest. Two days later the Khmer Rouge claimed the action, exaggerating the deaths. But we bumped across the hole left by the blast. We had no escort and there was civilian traffic in both directions. Closer to Thailand action is more considerable and insecurity a fact of life. But life is going on. In most villages, houses, schools or temples are being built. Perhaps the attitude of a restaurant woman summed it up. When asked about the insecurity, she described it as 'the sabotage of the defeated'.

The problems of today's Cambodia can only be registered adequately by taking a preliminary measure of the success encompassed by the Vietnamese-Khmer alliance. In the city, the main thing is the rejuvenation of elementary economic (if not yet manufacturing) activity. Its most visible aspect is the trade, especially in the glossy consumer goods from Thailand. Its basis lies as much in the good harvest of 1980, that was grown from Western aid seeds, distributed in part thanks to Soviet gasoline. A third factor has been just as remarkable, yet people tend to take it for granted: money. The new Cambodian riel was successfully

introduced in April 1980. It greatly stimulated production, both artisanal and the growth of cash crops. Officially the rate is four riels to the dollar; on the black market it is about 16. But the currency itself is acceptable even in large quantities. In February 1980, I reported that 'J' King of Freedom jeans could be acquired in the Phnom Penh markets only for gold. This time I was offered a pair for 250 riels. The rail fare to Battambang is 33 riels. Rice is two to three riels a kilo, a Khmer scarf 15 riels: the list could be extended, from Russian blankets to fake Khmer jewellery.

Down to the villages and hamlets, schoolteachers, minor officials, sons serving in the army, have a money wage as well as a rice ration. With cash crops such as tobacco and sesame seed, as well as the manufacture of mats and the drying of fish, an elementary economy, if not yet accumulation, is beginning in the rural areas. It is run politically by two parallel structures. Every district and sub-district within each province has its committee, recently 'elected' in a nationwide process. However subordinate, there is a functioning Khmer political machine, locally rooted and with a stake in the system. Alongside it is the Vietnamese army, garrisoned throughout the land. In the West, the troops engaged in fighting have been circulated, as a normal active army. But in the secure areas, a different pattern may emerge. We met one young soldier, the eldest son of a farming family from the outskirts of Saigon. He had been in Cambodia for three years, and, though a conscript, he accompanied some minor village officials. He was on his own and without a weapon. He spoke good Khmer himself now, wore a Khmer scarf, indeed only the emblem of a star on his hat distinguished him.

The Western media have often referred to Cambodia as 'Vietnam's Vietnam'. But the US relationship to Vietnam, when Washington invaded it, was notoriously ill-conceived. Troops often stayed for only six months and their main attitude to the Vietnamese was the 'body-count'; from male corpses to female prostitutes. The American Special Forces were supposedly closer to the people, but only in the way that a sado-masochist is 'closer' to his victim than a hit-and-run driver. In Cambodia most of the Vietnamese, like the Khmer, are peasants. They live at the same level as the Khmer, and alongside them. This is not to say that they are liked. But however feared, they are tolerated, and the evident intimacy means they are relatively well-informed and increasingly experienced. The Pol Pot forces, by contrast, seem hated and remote.

The most universally detested aspect of the Pol Pot regime, it emerges, was perhaps not the killings, nor the abolition of Buddhism, nor even forced labour, but rather the introduction of collective eating. No society, however utopian, treats all its citizens alike. Pol Pot, indeed, inflicted an extraordinary division on the countryside. All those deported from the towns, either genuinely urban classes or peasant refugees from the Lon Nol war, were categorised broadly as 'new people', while those who had stayed in the liberated zones were known as 'base people'. The 'new people' suffered much more under Pol Pot, they were far more subject to execution and to draconian labour conditions. Today, this has led to quite a sharp antagonism between town and country, with many of the educated resenting the peasantry. One government cadre told me that illiterate people should be feared 'as they have no sentiment'. But not all the 'new people' were city-educated. In one village in Prey Veng, we were told that about 30 per cent of the people there today had been 'new persons'; they had been rural refugees in Phnom Penh during the American war and were evacuated back to their villages when Pol Pot came to power in 1975. Twice stripped of their belongings, they still have nothing, and they remain the poorest by far in today's Cambodia. They have no draught animals for ploughing, no pigs for meat. A small hut, to shade them from the sun, may be inches from the water, or even under it. Without a dry mat or change of clothes, they have now suffered under three successive regimes. But they were *most* punished by Pol Pot's 'Democratic Kampuchea' and are hardly likely to support his return. The 'base people', on the other hand, had a somewhat better time but retain a degree of privilege. They have not lost their houses or animals, and many are now incorporated into the rural administration.

At the same time mutual aid teams seem to have won the acceptance of many villagers. These *Krom Samarki,* or solidarity groups, average a dozen families. Together they have an assigned number of hectares, which are farmed collectively, and whose produce is distributed according to work. The composition of the groups is mixed: they will include, say, a widow and two babies, without any animals or ploughs, and a surviving 'base' person and family with two oxen, plough and cart, i.e. the necessary instruments of production. In this way, the widow is assured of some food and income through participation in the *Krom Samarki,* while the more wealthy farmer can use his tools outside the collective land, for his own exclusive profit. In effect, the *Krom Samarki* function is an *ad hoc* insurance for the hardest hit victims of the 1970s.

If there is coherent opposition to the Vietnamese presence within Cambodia, its main concentration is in Phnom Penh, especially among government workers. Those who come into contact with Vietnamese authority, from schoolteachers obliged to cast historic relations between the two neighbours in a favourable light, to trained administrators from the Lon Nol and Sihanouk period, resent and may privately speak out against Hanoi.

My stay in Cambodia coincided with the meeting, in Singapore, between Sihanouk, his ex-premier and long time opponent Son Sann (both of whom claim military forces on the Thai border) and Khieu Samphan, nominal head of the Pol Pot group. The three signed a joint declaration of intent, to collaborate. If anything, it was greeted with relief in Phnom Penh itself. The government there has long been saying that Sihanouk was untrustworthy and in league with the West and the Chinese. Hor Nam Hong, the vice-Foreign Minister, now felt such propaganda to be vindicated, Sihanouk had denounced the Khmer Rouge for their 'barbaric genocide', he said; to sign a declaration with them was 'itself a crime'. The words were strong, but their delivery was, in this instance, calm. The Heng Samrin government has emerged as the only Khmer group unequivocally committed to the defeat of Pol Pot.

Its first major crisis is the forthcoming harvest. A double catastrophe of drought and rapid flooding has halved the potential harvest in many areas. Instead of increasing last year's crop, as the regime had hoped, some areas in the Southeast will suffer hunger. The deeper effects of war and revolution compound the problem, in a countryside savagely depleted of any savings. The aid agencies, led by the FAO, hope to boost the dry season crop with new rice strains and fertilizer; the paucity of the country's means, visible everywhere and always shocking, vindicates their renewed call for support. But what of the internal strains, those originating from Vietnam's victory in the war against Pol Pot?

In Phnom Penh, one of the more energetic Party leaders, who was trained in Vietnam and participated in the foundation of the anti-Pol Pot front, Keo Chanda, appears to have lost a round in some obscure leadership battle. Removed from the Ministry of Information and Culture to the key Ministry of Industry, he remains the Party secretary for Phnom Penh but without having been given a place on the Politbureau (or even, some say, on the Central Committee). Keo Chanda is one of the few Ministers with a popular style, it's said. Now it seems that Pen Sovan, the more remote Party chief, has moved on to diminish Keo Chanda's influence. On 2 September, Vietnam's independence day was celebrated, rather oddly, in Phnom Penh. It was a signal fact about the events of 1945 that Cambodia did not join forces with Vietnam in the general rising against colonial rule, one which swept most of Southeast Asia at the time. Nor in his famous Declaration of Independence that year, did Ho Chi Minh make any mention of Cambodia, Laos or 'Indochina'. Yet in 1981, it seems numerous Khmer government officials were gathered to stand under the hot sun all morning to solidarise with their neighbour's historic achievement.

On the 'Phnom' there are courting couples and geomancers with their charts. By the waterside, along the Mekong young men eat *Prong Teai Koun*. These are fertilised eggs, which contain the substance of an unhatched fledgling: the dark contents taste of meaty liver and juices. Prized for their concentrated energy, fertilised eggs are also believed to have an aphrodisiac quality. There was a peal of flirtatious laughter, from some young ladies made up and well dressed. My guide asked if I noticed they were Vietnamese, and he added that they had a different character to Kampucheans. 'They are more bold in attracting males', he explained, adding that Khmer girls were shy and retiring. I looked at the boys hanging about by the riverside; indubitably Khmer, drinking sugar cane juice in the sun, doubtless after a fertilised egg or two, and eyeing the prospects. What sort of takeover was this?

Cambodia: where you catch fish in bushes; where you eat meat out of eggs; where sugar comes from palm trees. You can sail across Cambodia, reported a mediaeval Chinese voyager to Angkor; even more so today when the waters are exceptionally high. When the peasants fled the stupendous constructions of Angkor they made a kind of pact with the flood waters and the sun. As its waters rise, the Mekong changes its direction and flows backwards *into* Cambodia—it is a basic fact about the country. The result is usually an all-encompassing, but relatively peaceful flooding that allows for shambolic, low-intensity rice cultivation with the minimum of earthworks and effort, and which brings fish and vegetables as well as timber. It's a gambler's paradise for peasants: they lose, but they laugh. Today the smiles (and the curses) have returned.

(25 September 1981)

Part IV
The bureaucracy of death

Tuol Sleng: Inside S 21
Anthony Barnett

'S 21' was the identification for what became the main interrogation centre of the
Pol Pot regime. Today it is known as Tuol Sleng. Here instruments of torture and
iron beds stained with human blood and waste, are on display. In a museum of
inhumanity, sunlight now fills what once were classrooms, and later reverberated
to screams. As in many museums, the human experience on record seems unreal.
In another room, a photographic display of mass graves which are surely authentic
includes two pictures, reproduced from the Western press, which are known to be
fabrications. There is, however, a vast mass of other evidence: the prison archives.

Nobody has suggested that the quantities of documents are not a genuine
product of Pol Pot's Democratic Kampuchea. There are arrest books, small sheets

Anthony Barnett

The document room at Tuol Sleng.

Khien Samphan, Sihanouk and Hu Nim.

typed out and stapled into months; day-sheets, recording the occupants by category; large sheets stapled at the top and headed *Chhmouk nak tous komtech*, literally 'the names of prisoners crushed to bits', followed by the date; and there are 'confessions'.

The Tuol Sleng complex consists of four large three-storey concrete buildings, with balcony corridors, which once had five classrooms on each floor, and a single-storey wooden building at the centre. Its name has caused some confusion. It was a Phnom Penh secondary school, built away from the main roads in the Sihanouk period. Then it was called Lycée Ponhea Yat. Under Lon Nol, its name was changed to Tuol Svay Prey. Next door, a primary school of other buildings was known as Tuol Sleng. And because that was the best known name for identifying its whereabouts, what next became 'S 21' is now called Tuol Sleng.

It is staffed by Khmer and headed by an ex-prisoner, Ung Pech. He survived because he was the prison's mechanic. Evacuated with the fleeing prison guards, he escaped and returned. He found the place vandalised, its records strewn about, many outside. (One of Hu Nim's confessions is damaged by what looks like rain and sun.) The archives are therefore seriously incomplete. Apparently they show that in 1975, 154 prisoners were taken in. For 1976, 2,250 are recorded. The figure rises to 6,330 for 1977, and to 5,765 for the first half of 1978 only. After that the records are lost. Thus a total of 14,449 prisoners has it seems been logged as entering S 21. Ung Pech reckons that there were also 2,000 children, and a considerable intake during the last half of 1978. The figure of 20,000 prisoners usually cited is therefore his estimate based on these projections.

The prison held an average of 1,000 to 1,500 at any one time. Stays there were short and almost always fatal. In October 1977 when the rate of exterminations accelerated, 179 were killed on the 18th, 88 on the 20th, and 148 on the 23rd. On the 15th, 418 were killed, the second highest daily total of all. The greatest single figure was 582, recorded on 27 May 1978; on other days, there were no executions. None of three 'day lists' selected at random recorded any. It seems that the condemned were gathered in lots over some time, and driven off together to be eliminated.

The two highest totals were all of soldiers from the Khmer Rouge Army, called back from the Eastern Region which borders on Vietnam. The prison was basically a political one, for personnel from the regime itself. But at least a thousand others have been recorded, and a full list of their names published. They include: 324 workers from various factories: 206 officers from the Sihanouk and Lon Nol Army; 113 teachers and professors; 87 foreigners, mainly Thai and Lao; 148 elite Khmer who returned from abroad; 194 students, and doctors and engineers as well. Many names are recorded of those who never saw Tuol Sleng, as one of the purposes of the confessions was to obtain lists of 'traitors'. Fantastic charts of 'lines' of contacts were then drawn up, in coloured inks.   (2 May 1980)

At the time of my visit, in February 1980, it seemed that much of the Tuol Sleng material was at risk and that, in a variety of ways, an invaluable if chilling record of the workings of the Pol Pot regime could be significantly depleted. I photographed and photocopied a small fragment of the records, which two Khmer scholars, Chanthou Boua and Ben Kiernan, analyse in the pages that follow. We instigated requests to fund a copying machine to be sent to the archive, to help ensure preservation and facilitate access by researchers. Eventually, scholarly institutions and aid agencies combined to achieve this, while the staff at Tuol Sleng improved their own searches and organisation. Thus even 'confessions' from late 1978, a

Hu Nim welcoming Sihanouk to the liberated areas of Cambodia, 1973.

period when records were thought to have been lost in their entirety (as noted above), have been uncovered: for example, the last testament of Vorn Vet, Pol Pot's economic minister who went down in one of the final purges. There remains a vast amount of information to be sifted before any definitive account of the central workings of the Pol Pot apparatus can be drawn up. But the photographs reproduced here, along with an examination of perhaps the longest handwritten set of confessions from a single individual, provided the first authenticated documentary proof of what was obvious, yet still surrounded by propaganda, self-deception and awkward minimisation: namely, proof of the deliberated, centralised character of the regime of terror created in Cambodia by Pol Pot, Ieng Sary and their associates. No American newspaper, magazine or journal of significant circulation, including those on the left, reproduced any of the material, however.

But a year later, a Washington journalist did confront Ieng Sary with the *New Statesman* of 2 May 1980. A description of the event concludes this section.

(September 1981)

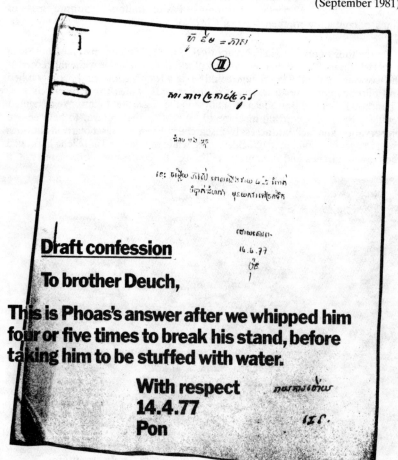

Draft confession

To brother Deuch,

This is Phoas's answer after we whipped him four or five times to break his stand, before taking him to be stuffed with water.

With respect
14.4.77
Pon

The 'confession' of Hu Nim

Little is known about the inner nature of Cambodia's Pol Pot dictatorship. A unique source of insight is the mass of records at Tuol Sleng, Pol Pot's interrogation centre. Here Chanthou Boua and Ben Kiernan analyse a small fraction of these records, brought out as photocopies by Anthony Barnett after his visit to Phnom Penh in 1980. The result is a chilling glimpse of a bureaucracy devoted to lethal megalomania: showing the need for full-scale examination—historical and psychological—of a political catastrophe with few modern parallels.

As our photographs show, many documents among the stacks of paper at Tuol Sleng are—or appear to be—'confessions'. They are mostly handwritten, in neat Khmer script, annotated here and there with details of the stages of torture which accompanied their compilation. The example dealt with here was chosen not exactly at random, but by a kind of guesswork.

Anthony Barnett doesn't read Khmer, a limitation he shares with all but a dozen Westerners, and nearly all Asians—Vietnamese included. Even given a time-schedule more lavish than a reporter can normally command, he would not have been able to sort and assess all of Tuol Sleng's semi-organised documents.

But he does have some knowledge of the recent politics of Cambodia—better called Kampuchea—and especially of the history of the left in that country. He therefore asked to see and copy the confession of Hu Nim, a politician of substance, who once served in Prince Sihanouk's cabinet before the exclusion of socialists in 1963.

He was one of three ex-Ministers who fled to the forests in 1967, and became the public leaders of the liberation movement after 1970. The other two were Hou Yuon and Khieu Samphan—the Chinese called them 'The Three People's Heroes', but the Americans denied their existence, and called them 'The Three Ghosts'. After 1975, Hu Nim became Information Minister in the communist government of Pol Pot. Someone in Barnett's position has to start with a name: in very rough parallel, an investigator surveying the archives of Stalinism might ask for the dossier of a Tukhachevsky or a Bukharin.

Hu Nim was listed as present at a banquet held in Phnom Penh to honour a Chinese delegation in January 1977. He was strangely absent from a similar

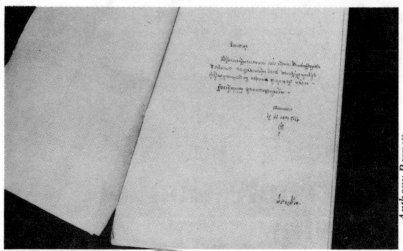

To brother Deuch,
This time the gist of Phoas's confession is that he hid other traitorous forces... He said that he is an independent CIA officer who buried himself for a long time, and did not carry out any impetuous anti-party activities, like those of the wicked Khoun and Ya groups.
I have tortured him to write it again.

With respect
22 April 1977
Pon

Prisoners had to rewrite their confessions. There were at least seven confessions by Hu Nim, written in the course of three months; this sheet was on the front of a shorter and earlier one.

gathering held on 17 April, the second anniversary of the fall of the city. Officially, he was supplanted as Information Minister in December 1977 by Yun Yat, wife of Defence Minister, Son Sann.

That step completed the political supremecy of four men (Pot Pot, Ieng Sary, Son Sann and Khieu Samphan) who had been Parisian students in the fifties, and of the women who married the first three of them (Yun Yat, Khieu Thirith and Khieu Ponnary—the latter two being sisters).

In December 1978 the American journalist Richard Dudman, visiting Phnom Penh, was told that Hu Nim was 'still active in government'. We now know that he was killed halfway through that year (his entry in the Tuol Sleng death-list is reproduced on page 126).

This year in Tuol Sleng Anthony Barnett was shown 'confessions' by Hu Nim totalling more than 200 pages. Each page is handwritten and signed. Thumbprints are attached to two of them, as our facsimile extract shows. These papers date from his arrest on 10 April to his execution on 6 July 1977.

In part, the confessions consist of a detailed autobiography, such that it would have been difficult for anyone but the man himself to have composed (he expresses, for instance, regret about sexual unfaithfulness to his wife: her name, it should be noted, occurs not long after his in the execution-lists). They are also partly the history of a particular, now notorious communist party.

But although many of the details are lifelike, and even interesting, the principal burden is obviously untrue—is fantastical, and grotesque. Hu Nim, apparently in his own hand, asserts that he was from 1957 onwards 'an officer of the CIA', directing every part of his life-work within the Kampuchean socialist movement towards

the construction of capitalism in Kampuchea... completely toeing the line of the American imperialists.

And in the same precise script he 'confesses' that

I'm not a human being, I'm an animal.

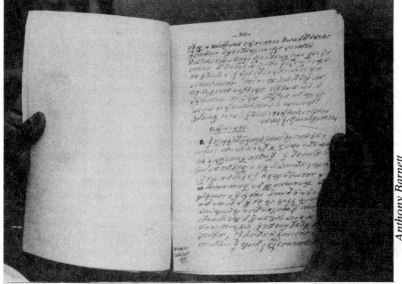

A page from Hu Nim's confession held up for the camera by one of Pol Pot's torture victims (see disfigured thumb).

Plainly the significance of such a document is not the credibility of its central proposition. Hu Nim, like most politicians, had his ambiguities—although most of the evidence about him suggests that his essential allegiance was to a kind of nationalist Maoism. The idea that he might have intrigued with Hanoi against an official Kampuchean regime is not absurd: and although he would have been as implausible as any other Khmer nationalist in the role of a Vietnamese agent, he might plausibly have committed some error or betrayal sufficient to earn a bullet in his head from one or other of the factions involved in the Indochinese wars.

But when he writes of himself as a cunning, lifelong CIA officer, of entirely undetectable duplicity ('The people saw me as a "progressive", a "leftist". In fact, deep in my mind...') he shows that what existed at Tuol Sleng was an organisation which could extract any desired confession from almost anyone.

That Pol Pot ran a violent, repressive regime is something scarcely open to question. Indeed, many of those who justify doing business with its remnants often by way of attacks upon the Vietnamese who overturned it—start from this point. There is a right-wing argument which suggests that Pol Pot and his friends, while ferocious, were not more so than any other rough, tough Third World government. And there is a left-wing argument—once held, evidently, by Noam Chomsky—which suggests that, although Pol Pot made numerous brutal errors, the conception of something especially outlandish about his regime is a chimera bred-up by the Western (and Vietnamese) news-media. Also, of course, there is the fact that most of the Kampuchean coverage which the newspapers can now provide is devoted, properly enough, to the question of whether or not another famine can be avoided. Complex, remote and unfamiliar, Kampuchea has slipped down the list of fashionable tragedies.

But Hu Nim's 'confession', together with some of the other documents reproduced here—the slaughter lists, the daily prison returns, the insane diagrams representing notional CIA and KGB 'subversion'—may reassert the point that there was something entirely bizarre about the Pol Pot regime.

Bizarre, yet disturbingly familiar in parts. Here is a section of Hu Nim's confession, purportedly describing his relations with party workers in 1968, during the days of guerrilla warfare:

> One day Comrade Sau and I had a discussion... (he) asked me: 'You used to live... in the Western world. What was their system, their way of life, their development like?'
> Because I was a CIA officer, traitor to the party, the people, I took that opportunity to influence Comrade Sau. In fact the capitalist system brings suffering to the poor, the workers and the peasants, and provides happiness to only a handful of capitalists. But I used my cheap traitorous concept and told Comrade Sau that 'there were great developments in capitalist countries, especially in technical fields. Farmers... plough with tractors. They use machines for everything. And they have freedom... Nowadays, the world has a tendency towards capitalism.'

Tractors especially were hate-objects to the Pol Pot regime, because they exemplified the corruptions of foreign technology: even a decade-old conversation referring to their usefulness could be a traitorous act. But whatever the particular item, this relentless coughing up of yesterdays evokes a very specific memory; that of the Stalinist treason trials, and of subsequent epidemics of forced recantation. And the confessional minutiae are accompanied by something else which has been seen before: total psychological prostration, and the surrender of every trace of personal judgement. Hu Nim writes:

> For the past one-and-a-half months, I have received lots of education from the Party. I have nothing to depend on, I have only the Communist Party of Kampuchea. Would the party please show clemency towards me. My life is completely dependent upon the party.
> If there is anything wrong in this report will the party please show clemency.
> With the most profound respect.   28/5/77

A few weeks after this, his name appears in an execution-list.

The man who wrote this confession was about 48, and had been politically engaged since his high-school days, when he joined the 'People's Movement', a group of middle-class youths opposed to French colonialism. As a journalist—one holding a PhD in law—and a notably talkative intellectual, he was no doubt easily portrayed in the latter stages of the Pol Pot nightmare as a born class-enemy.

But the suggestion that Pol Pot's clique represented peasant purity against corrupt bourgeois values should not be taken too seriously. Pol Pot, who surfaced from an almost totally mysterious background in 1976, described himself as coming from a 'poor peasant' family: in fact, he appears to be a relative of the Khmer royal family.

It took some time after his rise to power to discover that Pol Pot's original name was Saloth Sar.

A refugee named Laau Thuok, now working in Paris, recalls that during his own boyhood in the thirties Saloth Sar lived in the next-door village. He knew Sar 'very well... we often played together as boys'. Sar's father, he says, was a landowner 'with a name' in the area. He had a cousin who was one of the principal wives of King Monivong (1927-41) and a sister who was a royal concubine with a court title. His brother, Saloth Chhay, was employed in the royal palace at Phnom Penh. And Thuok says that at one point in the thirties the king visited Saloth Sar's family in their village. There is no doubt much more to be discovered about the curious kin-relationships among Kampuchean politicians: but the suggestion of any straight split between peasantry and bourgeois would be an heroic oversimplification.

Knowledge of Hu Nim, apart from that which may be gained through the strange distorting-glass of his confession, is scanty enough itself. After the French granted independence, he studied for two years in Paris. In 1957 he was elected to the National Assembly. He travelled to the Soviet Union and Eastern Europe, and although his confession states that his aim then was one of 'changing the line of the Communist Party of Kampuchea... into a revisionist party and movement', he took conspicuous stands against 'revisionism' in the Soviet Union, and moved steadily towards the Chinese 'anti-revisionst' ideas which exploded in the Cultural Revolution.

He spent a month in China on the eve of the Cultural Revolution in 1965—to the fury of Prince Sihanouk, who had already expelled Hu Nim from the cabinet. Together with Phouk Chhay, he was the leader of the anti-revisionist movement in Phnom Penh and other towns. Sihanouk accused them of 'attacking the Soviet Union without reason', and during the next couple of years Sihanouk's attacks on Hu Nim became, in effect, denunciations of him as a *Chinese* front-man:

> Phouk Chhay is the fiercest among this handful of people who aid China. The most dissolute and dishonest is Hu Nim... (they) have excluded themselves from the national community...

There is dizzying lunacy in the idea that Hu Nim was undertaking all this pro-Chinese, pro-Maoist campaigning on behalf of the *CIA*. It was years before the rapprochement between Mao and the Americans: by the time Hu Nim came to 'confess' that this was so, he was confessing it to people whose own principal supporters were the Chinese, and (indirectly) the Americans. Sihanouk's verbal assaults turned into a direct, unmistakable threat by October 1967:

> I consider Hu Nim and his associates as traitors, and they will be subjected to the military tribunal and the execution block.

Two days later, Hu Nim slipped away from his house, went into the jungle, and became one of the Three Heroes (or Ghosts). The confession gives elaborate detail of how he spent the next few years scheming towards the restoration of

Anthony Barnett

capitalism in Kampuchea—but the outside world, of course, had little knowledge of Hu Nim until he emerged with the victorious Khmer Rouge leadership after the fall of Phnom Penh in 1975.

There is no evidence that 'Maoists' like Hu Nim and Phouk Chhay opposed the spectacular evacuation of Phnom Penh in 1975 and the rurally-based radicalism that provided its ideological justification. Indeed, refugees have reported having seen him chatting to the evacuees on their way out of the city.

Internal evidence from the confession suggests that his doubts began to grow at the end of 1976, or the start of 1977—when Pol Pot began to introduce compulsory collective eating, administrative purges down to village level, and simultaneous attempts to eliminate all senior party opponents. He writes that he found himself 'disturbed and tormented' by theoretical documents about collectivism produced at a party study session. Still

> my strategy was that if I violently, openly and frontally opposed the party, I could not succeed in my main aim.

This is one of the points where his 'main aim' is not specified, and is not attached to grotesqueries about 'toeing the line of the imperialists'. It is one of the most tantalising sections of the document: for it seems as though under the tortured, lunatic superstructure of 'confession' one can discern some shadowy narrative telling the story of the Kampuchean communists' resistance to Pol Pot.

That resistance was utterly destroyed—'crushed to bits'—by the relentless machinery of Tuol Sleng. Yet, just as the dreadful records of the Gestapo give, here and there, some clues as to the nature of the people they destroyed, there may be more information about the liquidated opposition buried away in the 11,000-or-so confessions and dossiers which lie in Tuol Sleng awaiting investigation.

And indeed there are traces of this resistance which can be picked up from other

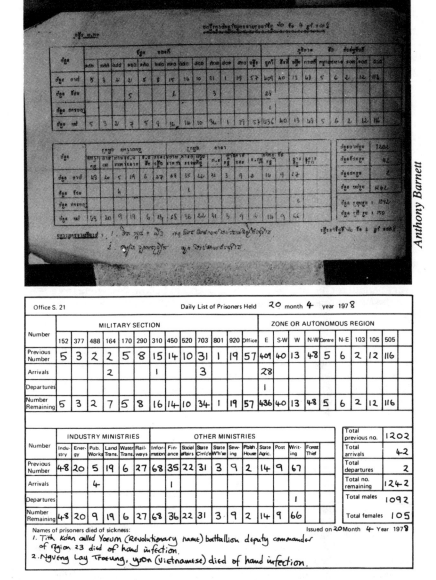

Anthony Barnett

Office S. 21													Daily List of Prisoners Held		20	month	4	year 1978				
Number	MILITARY SECTION														ZONE OR AUTONOMOUS REGION								
	152	377	488	164	170	290	310	450	520	703	801	920	Office	E	S-W	W	N-W	Centre	N-E	103	105	505
Previous Number	5	3	2	2	5	8	15	14	10	31	1	19	57	409	40	13	48	5	6	2	12	116
Arrivals			2				1			3				28								
Departures														1								
Number Remaining	5	3	2	7	5	8	16	14	10	34	1	19	57	436	40	13	48	5	6	2	12	116

Number	INDUSTRY MINISTRIES						OTHER MINISTRIES											Total previous no.	1202
	Industry	Energy	Pub. Works	Land Trans.	Water Trans.	Railways	Information	Finance	Social affairs	State Cm'ce	State W'h'se	Sewing	Pbish. House	State Agric.	Post	Writing	Forest Thief		
																		Total arrivals	42
Previous Number	48	20	5	19	6	27	68	35	22	31	3	9	2	14	9	67		Total departures	2
Arrivals			4					1										Total no. remaining	1242
Departures																1		Total males	1092
Number Remaining	48	20	9	19	6	27	68	36	22	31	3	9	2	14	9	66		Total females	105

Names of prisoners died of sickness: Issued on 20 Month 4 Year 1978
1. Tith Kdan called Yaeum (Revolutionary name) battallion deputy commander of region 23 died of hand infection.
2. Nguyen Lay Troeung, ypon (Vietnamese) died of hand infection.

Prison officers filled in a duplicated 'day sheet' of the number of prisoners held, by category. They were broken down by military unit, region and State Ministry. The sheet reproduced and translated above was taken at random from the pile on the office table shown opposite.

sources. Some time ago a Khmer Rouge defector to Thailand reported that around 1976-77 'several members of the party such as Hu Nim and Nhim asked the party to have mercy on the people, saying that the party must act to carry out democratic actions according to the democratic system. They said that working people must not be persecuted, and foreign aid must be accepted so that the Kampuchean people do not suffer too much. Such opinions were regarded by the party as subversion...'

It is reasonable to estimate that Hu Nim was one of these 'subversives'. We don't know what was different about him and his fellow-objectors. They had, after all, passed through as much war and bloodshed as the rest of the party leadership: witnessed, and presumably sanctioned terrible deeds and events. (The long columns of Phnom Penh evacuees with whom Hu Nim was seen conversing in 1975 included sick and wounded who were literally walking to their deaths.) But there was apparently something in them which revolted against the proposition that killing and repression, once begun, should simply continue until a whole population—or its remnant—could be fitted into one unyielding social and moral framework.

What is clear is that for Hu Nim's interrogators it was crucially necessary to establish that this was an ideological flaw present in him from the beginning. Even the People's Movement which he joined at Sisowath High School had to be

> a traitorous movement which the American imperialist firstly formed as an instrument of aggression against the nation and people of Kampuchea... It is very painful for me that when I was 22 years old I chose this wrong road. It is this first wrong road that determined my future in life and politics for 25 years...

While he was in the People's Movement the future Maoist succumbed to a remarkable, and indeed quite inconsistent set of ideological infections. He became 'prone to private property', and was seized by 'a concept and standpoint (that) was petty bourgeois, *capitalist* and *feudalist*' (emphasis added: the idea of a capitalist feudalist would have astounded Marx).

But this was only the preparation for a formal enlistment into the service of the Americans. Not long after his return from study in France, Hu Nim set out to become a member of the Legislative Assembly, which meant joining the Popular Socialist Community, the only vehicle possible at the time. He was introduced to the party by two of its existing members—one of whom, Mau Say, was on this confessional evidence an officer of the CIA, and used the occasion to induct Hu Nim into that service. Purportedly Hu Nim 20 years later had a perfect recollection of the almost Masonic formulation employed:

> Mau Say... laid down the conditions, saying: 'Both of us will agree to act as referees for you to join the Popular Socialist Community... and accord you status, on condition that you follow our leadership and all our orders, as an officer of the CIA, serving the activities of the CIA, serving American imperialism and opposing communism... and successfully heading towards the construction of capitalism in Kampuchea, completely toeing the line of the Free World and the American imperialists...'

But for all this secret pledging, the young journalist-politician appears not to have committed any overt acts of imperialism such as might be confessed to—even under torture—two decades later. Therefore the confession manufactures fierce rhetoric about the difference between his outward socialism and his deeply-buried motives:

> On the surface it seemed that I was a 'total revolutionary', as if I was 'standing on the people's side'... If the people listened to my speeches on the open parliamentary platform about 'opposing American imperialism and its lackeys', it sounded very sharp. But in fact, deep in my mind, the essence was service of the American imperialists... I wrote a thesis for my law doctorate which even took a progressive stand (on reform of economic administration)... These were the cheapest acts which hid my reactionary, traitorous, corrupted elements, representing the feudalist, capitalist, imperialist establishment and the CIA...

For a simple murder, of course, nothing but convenience is necessary. But in order to justify the liquidation of a well-known public figure, and indeed a 'People's Hero', something more than this kind of induced rhetoric must be obtained. Having established Hu Nim as a CIA officer, the confession moves on, gathers up one or two shreds of what may be genuine fact, and conjures up the outline of a lethal accusation: the formation of an illegitimate and secret party-within-the-party. This was the 'Marxist-Leninist Party' of Kampuchea, named so 'as to make it easier to gather forces from the left, right and centre'. It was constituted, Hu Nim told his interrogators, in order to

> ... seize power and rule Kampuchea in the form of a capitalist state within the framework of the Free World... operational methods were—to gather all possible forces, including the Pracheachon group*, in order to succeed in the above aim;—to bury ourselves inside the Communist Party of Kampuchea—to change the line of the KPC... into a revisionist party and movement...

However, this lethal conspiracy never had more than three members, and existed for only one meeting. During 1967, Hu Nim records, the Khmer-Chinese Friendship Association mounted an exhibition of Chinese cultural and artistic works. Two friends of Hu Nim's helped organise the exhibition—Phouk Chhay, co-target of Sihanouk's denunciations, and Van Tep Sovan—and he met them during the course of it. He then 'confesses' that they formed a party on the spot, although

> as for the administration, there was no secretary yet, because it was the first meeting.

It was also the last, because almost immediately Sihanouk issued his threat, and the flight to the jungle began. Quite soon Phouk Chhay was arrested and Van Tep Sovan killed: thus the 'Marxist-Leninist Party of Kampuchea'—probably, outside of a torturer's imagination, nothing more than a political discussion between three friends—came to an end.

Yet it preserves, for confessional purposes, a weird and ghostly existence. Three years later, in the *maquis*, the People's Hero Hu Nim meets another

---

* The Pracheachon (Citizens) group was a communist organisation—semi-legal under Sinahouk—made up of veterans of the Viet-Minh-supported Kampuchean resistance to the French, 1946-54. Because of their Vietnamese connections, Pracheachon members were among the Pol Pot regime's primary targets.

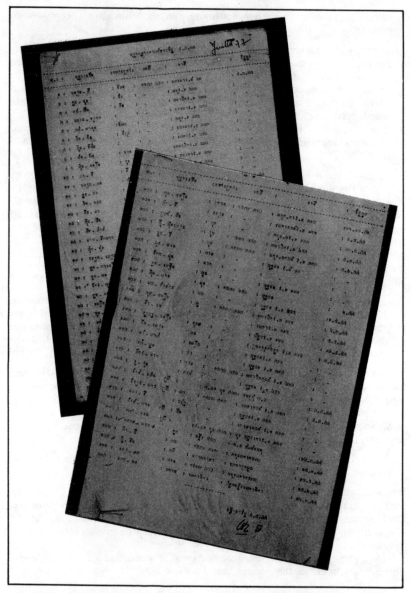

'*Prisoners crushed to bits: 6 July 1977*' *reads the heading to this list of 127 victims which include Cambodian student leader Phouk Chhay and Pol Pot's former Minister of Information Hu Nim. The signature is illegible.*

undercover CIA officer, the notorious traitor 'Khuon' (real name Koy Thuon, and since executed). In stilted, conspirational tones they discuss its possible merger with Khuon's 'Workers' Party', a body of little, if any, greater substance:

> (Khuon said): 'When you formed it in 1967 there were only three of you... you are the only one left. If you want to dissolve it into our Workers' Party, that is all right... It's up to you.'
> I answered Khuon immediately: 'It would be very good to merge them together because the two parties have only one aim, i.e. to overthrow the Communist Party of Kampuchea, seize power and rule Kampuchea in the form of a capitalist country, completely toeing the line etc'.

Yet there are patches where something recognisable as the life of a guerrilla politician engaged in a terrifying war comes across. He recalls 1973 as 'the year that the (US) enemies waged a big war in Kampuchea. All types of airplanes including the dreadful B-52s dropped bombs which shook the land and shook the water...' The work of a propaganda office in the 'liberated zone' (apparently Hu Nim's responsibility) consisted to a considerable extent of helping the soldiers keep the slit-trenches in good repair.

Whether as a make-weight to add to a confession clearly lacking in concrete acts of imperialism, or as a device for the erosion of self-respect, Hu Nim was made to acknowledge sexual betrayal as well (of course, the Pol Pot regime was concerned to impose an iron chastity):

> I would like to tell the party that when I got back to the liberated zone (in 1971) I was aroused by a woman and was unfaithful to my wife. At that time she was very sick and I took her to the hospital...
> I betrayed her, who loved me as much as her own life: while she yet lived, I asked a peasant girl from the south-west to marry me... I hurt myself very much with this big mistake. I was a traitor to the party and also to my family...

Quite what to make of this is not clear. Apparently nothing came of the peasant marriage, and clearly Hu Nim's wife survived her illness—to be executed eventually in Tuol Sleng.

Opening a new section, Hu Nim writes: 'I would now like to tell the party about my traitorous activities after the liberation' (as Minister of Information). These again are essentially insubstantial, but conjured to sound impressive—and the mysterious authority-figures of 'Brother No. 1' and 'Brother No. 2' begin to appear.

He meets Khuon and discusses the business of feeding radio performers. 'I told him we ate according to the Organisation's rules... lacking vegetables, meat and fish':

> Khuon then said: 'You must feed the performers well, otherwise they can't work...'
> From the following day Khuon sent a carload of vegetables, fish and meat to the artistic group every morning. And from then on I allowed male and female performers to go... to meet Khuon all the time. So I am a traitor to the party, I am a traitor to the party's secrecy policy, a traitor to the Organisation's instructions which forbid people to contact one another and do not permit people to go in and out from one Ministry to another without permission.

It seems to be significant that the Tuol Sleng prison-return forms (one is reproduced on p.123) were based on the proportions of prisoners held from each
government department. Connections, as the strange 'network' charts show, were
one obsession of Pol Pot's regime. And resistance to the national policy of
seclusion and monasticism was building up by 1976. Hu Nim admits to knowing
about the first meetings, though apparently he was not caught up in the 'network'.
Brother Nhim, who did not agree with the 'self-reliance policy', and wanted to
obtain 'materials, machinery and tractors from other countries', held a meeting in
Phnom Penh with brothers Phim, Khuon and Doeun, where they agreed to

> rule Kampuchea as a revisionist country like Vietnam, toeing the line of the
> Soviet Union, and accepting aid from all countries... especially the United
> States...
>   Later the Organisation took measures to deal with Khuon (after he had
> committed a moral transgression with a woman). Brother No. 2... told us about
> (Khuon's) corrupt history... The Organisation had tried very hard to educate
> Khuon, but he had never changed.

'Brother No. 1' is fairly certainly Pol Pot, and 'No. 2' very likely to be Ieng Sary.
Why numbers? Merely to be *named*—however peripherally—in one of these
confessions appears to have led directly to inclusion in a 'network', arrest, torture,
confession in turn, and execution. There was perhaps good reason for the masters
of the Organisation to keep their own names secluded from the process.
   The year 1977 began with 'Prom Sam Ar hanging himself'. Hu Nim says that he
was much 'disturbed' by policy sessions run for 'the core of the Organisation',
about

> ... class positions in the new Kampuchean society... about materialism, about
> the abolition of money, about popular education... It disturbed and tormented
> most those individuals who were prone to private property and had strong
> middle-class, feudalist and capitalist standpoints.

Then 'Brother No. 1' requested a 'new orientation in broadcasting', asking that
'the building of socialism be pushed very strongly by broadcasting about models.'
These models were to be regions of Kampuchea of which 'No. 1' approved:
especially Kompong Chhnang, 'where they use no machinery at all, only labour'.
Kompong Chhnang, said 'Brother No. 1', was supporting the state much more
than the Northern or Northwestern zones:

> After listening to Brother No. 1 I saw great shortcomings in my past work,
> because we had spoken well of both zones... in texts as well as songs. The
> declaration of Brother No. 1... made me realise that Nhim's stand, for a system
> of plenty, was a great deal different from the party line. But I did not report it to
> Brother No. 1 because I was already a traitor.

Just what happened next is obscure. Apparently Hu Nim tried to reach the
Northwest zone, to speak to Nhim, by travelling with a visiting North Korean film
unit. But he was recalled to Phnom Penh, where he heard that the Organisation
was making numerous arrests. He says:

> I would like to tell the party, with respect:
>   After Brother No. 2 had two work meetings with me, the last day being 10
> April 1977, I gave myself to the party.

From then on I have been doing self-criticism every day. I see that my criminal acts against the Organisation, against the Communist Party of Kampuchea, against the nation and people of Kampuchea, are of great dimension.

After thanking the party for 'lots of education', he makes his fruitless appeal for clemency, and appends a list of 91 other 'traitors'. He was 'crushed to bits' on the same day as Phouk Chhay; given the maniac precision of the system, this could hardly be fortuitous.

(2 May 1980)

Don't blame me, it was my brother-in-law

Anthony Barnett

It was a choice moment in the annals of crime. A man with direct responsibility for some of the worst mass killings of our epoch, was presented with direct evidence of the deed. Ieng Sary was shown a copy of the *New Statesman*.

Elizabeth Becker interviewed Ieng Sary in New York in July 1981. He was there to attend the United Nations as the recognized representative of the Cambodian people. She handed him an issue of the *New Statesman* dated 2 May 1980. On its cover was a photograph of the note attached to a 'draft confession'. In Khmer handwriting it said:

> To brother Deuch, this is Phoas's answer after we whipped him four or five times to break his stand, before taking him to be stuffed with water. With respect, Pon.

The note was dated 14 April 1977. Phoas was the political name of Hu Nim, Ieng Sary's colleague who had been Minister of Information of the Pol Pot government. Ieng Sary, Pol Pot's brother-in-law, was its Foreign Minister.

Ieng Sary put on his spectacles. The poor chap's eyesight is now giving him trouble. 'Yes, that is true,' he told Becker. 'Deuch, head of security,' and he turned over the pages to authenticate the mass of documentation assembled in an eight-page spread.

What was Ieng Sary's explanation? 'We were in the middle of class struggle', the 'circumstances' were ones of 'proletarian dictatorship'. Pol Pot 'knew the accused were killed'. 'Personally I wasn't aware of the deaths'.

He did not deny knowledge of the confessions. Elsewhere, he has expressed knowledge of the contents of one, made by another senior colleague. Perhaps he thought that after being broken, the victims were sent to a health farm. Yet he expressed neither surprise nor remorse when Becker pointed out the full-page illustration of a single day's execution list, with the names of 127 victims, which was headed: 'Prisoners crushed to bits, 6 July 1977'.

Recently copies of parts of another confession have arrived in the West, that of Sokhom Hing. He was the leading 'Front' representative in New York and the chief UN lobbyist for the Cambodian revolutionaries prior to their victory in 1975. He was sent back home by Thiounn Prasit. Today Prasit is the permanent representative in New York, the man the British government votes to keep in its company. Instead of receiving three months' training, as Prasit promised, Sokhom Hing went straight to a forced labour 'collective' and, when his three months were up, to Tuol Sleng.

There, in October 1976, he confessed that during his labours he tried to get others

> to adopt a revisionist line in working, in eating, in morale, in attitude. For example, promoting the idea of wanting to eat different kinds of food, different kinds of dresses, revisionism in food... I would always talk a lot, joke a lot, about this, about that... to slow down the work. This was a betrayal of the revolutionary organization which tries to promote the country's construction movement.

Two days before he had already confessed:

> I like to talk about having sweet rice soup, or think about making different kinds of cakes for the memorial day for the dead, especially before I came to this interrogation centre.

Two months later, according to the prison files, he was exterminated.

The next time the world's diplomats rub shoulders with Ieng Sary at UN receptions, as the US Secretary of State did the other day, perhaps they should spare a thought for Sokhom Hing, while they savour the canapés.

(7 August 1981)

Part V
The
United Nations

The Pol Pot Fan Club: still open for business
Anthony Barnett

In 1979, when the United Nations first voted to recognise the Pol Pot regime of Democratic Kampuchea as the legitimate representative of Cambodia, diplomats said that it would not happen again. It did. In 1980 and 1981 the endorsement was repeated, with diminishing publicity in the media, as governments in the West strove to play down 'embarrassing' coverage of what they were doing. The UN vote of 'principle' became even more of a farce through the activity of the Democratic Kampuchean delegation which, as a full member of the Assembly, may influence that body's decisions. In a vote on the question of East Timor, in 1980, Ieng Sary's subordinates endorsed the Indonesian position. Indonesia at present occupies the whole of East Timor and has brazenly incorporated that country into a province, in the process annihilating at least a quarter of the population. Thus a regime branded as 'genocidal' gave its support to an ongoing policy of genocide, having previously supported East Timor's independence.

The reports which follow cover the UN vote of 1980, in which Britain did indeed vote as forecast, the UN Conference on Cambodia, held in July 1981, and list the distribution of votes in 1980 along with the few shifts that took place a year later.

BRITAIN VOTES FOR GENOCIDE
The British government is going to vote for Pol Pot at the United Nations. That is the meaning of Lord Carrington's obscurely-phrased address to the General Assembly here on 23 September 1980. 'The stand taken by the countries of the Association of Southeast Asian Nations (ASEAN) has my government's full support.' That stand is to endorse the Pol Pot regime as the legitimate representative of the Khmer people, and to re-arm and re-supply its forces in Thailand, an ASEAN country.

The foreign minister of Singapore, the most active ASEAN spokesman on this issue, told the General Assembly that Pol Pot's nationalist cause was 'just' and should be backed with all the 'moral force' of a UN vote. According to the representative of a major Third World country that will abstain as it did last year, 'the Americans and the Chinese have lined up their constituencies', and the ASEAN lobby has firmed up those who seemed to falter—including Lord Carrington.

The British will embrace Pol Pot 'with a heavy heart', a spokesman conceded when he confirmed the policy. The equivalent American phrase is 'we will hold our nose'. Both would prefer the matter to go through without the embarrassment of a vote. But at least the US Secretary of State, Muskie, told his public outright what his administration had decided. The British are lying doggo. At his press conference Lord Carrington slipped from Afghanistan to Namibia in his list of problems to be solved, without a mention of Kampuchea, so as not to provoke a question. None came. As credentials are usually uncontroversial and unchallenged, the British hope that the specific responsibility of a recorded assent to Pol Pot can be evaded.

The meeting of the credentials committee on 22 September, here at the UN, held out some hope for this manoeuvre. Behind its relatively brief and casual proceedings lay an extraordinary amount of scheming and argument: many hours of preparation for an event of less than sixty minutes. The journal of the UN's daily events did not say the meeting would be a closed one, and a television camera and lights had been set up in the small conference room. As the delegates gathered outside, however, the wires were pulled and the camera wheeled away. The as yet unconvinced committee had 'decided' to proceed in private (nobody asked me to leave).

There was an atmosphere of quiet bonhomie as delegates wandered in and greeted each other—although this did not extend to relations between the Chinese and Soviets. Rather absurdly, both the US delegates sported red ties, a dash of colour upstaged only by the glittering suit worn by the man from Singapore. A younger and earnest member of the Chinese delegation spoke rapidly and purposefully to the Americans, then left and returned behind the two older and senior Chinese spokesmen who did not share his fluent English. There are nine members of the committee. In a small semi-circle sat Kenya, Singapore, Spain, the USSR, the United States, Costa Rica (which was given the chair), Angola, China and Haiti.

Ieng Sary wandered in, podgy, impassive and (here) respectable: Pol Pot's vice prime minister, foreign minister and brother-in-law. The Chinese spokesman opened the proceedings. He moved that Pol Pot's government was the sole legal government of Kampuchea, one which led its people and army in its resistance to aggression. The Soviets responded by supporting Heng Samrin's revolutionary council and denouncing Pol Pot for committing 'the worst possible crimes' against the Cambodian people. Angola spoke next: the people in Cambodia had themselves already rejected the credentials of the Pol Pot gang, its representative pointed out—an argument which is evidently irrefutable. Nonetheless, the US delegate who followed said his government found Pol Pot's credentials to be 'in order'. Then Ambassador Koh of Singapore took the floor and enjoyed himself with a cynical performance (of which more later). Finally, Haiti spoke up, echoing the formulation of the United States: despite 'practices counter to the recognition of human rights' the delegation from the previously accredited regime was acceptable. The alliance between voodoo dictatorship and born-again democracy clinched the proceedings. In a prepared move the chairman composited the Chinese motion, which specifically endorsed Pol Pot, into a resolution that recognised the entire list of credentials of the countries put forward by Waldheim's office. This passed without objection. The matter now goes before the General Assembly. The Vietnamese say that they are willing to allow for delays, and thereby leave the matter open, for they fear a vote will make things more inflexible. For the same reason, Ieng Sary is pushing for a decision, and that, the Vietnamese insist, will not take place without a full debate and a named vote on the specific issue of Cambodia.

It is generally felt that their most formidable adversary will be Singapore's fluent ambassador. In the credentials committee he too ignored the Angolan argument and said that there could be 'no justifiable political reason' for rejecting Pol Pot's credentials. Singapore had always condemned his human rights record, he said, unlike the Soviets and the Vietnamese, who only discovered these excesses after they invaded: 'much to their surprise, I am sure'. The Chinese delegates especially appreciated that joke, and laughed knowingly to each other as Ambassador Koh accused the Russians of shedding 'crocodile tears'. As we all left the room a UN official could be heard congratulating Koh on his 'good speech'. Apart from the fact that Hanoi was denouncing Pol Pot's internal policies for a year prior to the invasion, the logic of Koh's position is rather strange. In effect he said 'You were atrociously unprincipled then, so you can't complain if we are now equally unprincipled in turn'.

There is no purpose served in arguing the case with such spokesmen or taking seriously their selective application of 'principle'. Why does the West endorse Pol Pot? Why does it condemn an invasion which most Cambodians accepted with relief? Not because of any attachment to natural sovereignty, surely, but because of disappointment that the Vietnamese, not the West itself or its allies, did the deed. Nobody doubts that if Thailand had ousted Pol Pot its forces would be in Cambodia today *and* its client regime would be seated now in the United Nations.

A vote for Pol Pot is justified as one against Heng Samrin, who people feel sure would eventually fill a vacant seat if the assembly decided now to oust the 'odious' incumbents. In fact, if the vote is not in favour of Pol Pot and is also against Heng Samrin, then the West is really arguing for Son Sann, the rightwing Cambodian leader presently building up forces in Thailand. This is the man who headed Sihanouk's national bank, and who the US now considers should have replaced him in 1970, instead of Lon Nol. Thus the vote for Pol Pot symbolises an attempt to re-write the United States' war in Southeast Asia, with continuing disregard for the life and hopes of the people of Cambodia.

(3 October 1980)

STAND UP AND BE COUNTED
For the seating of Pol Pot

Argentina, Australia, Bahamas, Bahrain, Barbados, Bangladesh, Belgium, Bhutan, Bolivia, Cameroons, Canada, Chile, China, Colombia, Comoros, Costa Rica, Democratic Kampuchea, Denmark, Djibouti, Dominican Republic, Ecuador, Egypt, El Salvador, Equitorial Guinea, Fiji, Gabon, Gambia, Germany (West), Greece, Guatemala, Haiti, Honduras, Indonesia, Israel, Italy, Japan, Kenya, Kuwait, Lesotho, Liberia, Luxembourg, Malaysia, Maldives, Malta, Mauritania, Mauritius, Morocco, Nepal, New Zealand, Niger, Nigeria, Oman, Pakistan, Papua New Guinea, Paraguay, Philippines, Portugal, Qatar, Saudi Arabia, Senegal, Singapore, Somalia, Sri Lanka, Sudan, Thailand, Togo, Turkey, UK, USA, Upper Volta, Uruguay, Venezuela, Yugoslavia, Zaire.
TOTAL: 74

Abstained
Austria, Botswana, Brazil, Burundi, Central African Republic, Chad, Finland,
France, Ghana, Iceland, Ireland, Ivory Coast, Lebanon, Mali, Mexico, Nether-
lands, Norway, Peru, Rwanda, Samoa, Sierra Leone, Spain, Surinam, Sweden,
Trinidad & Tobago, Tunisia, Uganda, United Arab Emirates, Tanzania, Yemen,
Zambia, Zimbabwe.
TOTAL: 32

No vote recorded
Burma, Cyprus, Dominica, Iran, Iraq, Jordan, Malawi, Romania, Saint Lucia, St
Vincent & the Grenadines, Solomon Islands, Swaziland.
TOTAL: 12

Against the seating of Pol Pot
Afghanistan, Albania, Algeria, Angola, Benin, Bulgaria, Byelorussia, Cape
Verde, Congo, Cuba, Czechoslovakia, Democratic Yemen, Ethiopia, Germany
(East), Grenada, Guinea, Guinea-Bissau, Guyana, Hungary, India, Jamaica,
Laos, Libya, Madagascar, Mongolia, Mozambique, Nicaragua, Panama, Poland,
St Tome & Principe, Seychelles, Syria, Ukraine, USSR, Vietnam.
TOTAL: 35

(24 October 1980)

THE UNITED NATIONS SPECIAL CONFERENCE
Speaking in the congenial milieu of Peking's new America Club, John Holdridge
announced on 17 June 1981 that the United States would increase 'military
pressure on Vietnam'. The Holdridge Declaration, otherwise known as the Haig
Doctrine of 'Arms across the Pacific', was promptly assailed by the *Washington
Post*. The rest of America, including its 'Left', seemed incapable of paying
attention.

Holdridge is the new Assistant Secretary for East Asia and he accompanied
Haig to China for talks with Deng Xiaoping. His remarks at the American Club
were carefully chosen. 'We will seek', he said modestly, without presuming
success, 'to find ways to increase the political, economic, and yes, military pres-
sures on Vietnam, working with others in ways which will bring about, we hope,
some change in Hanoi's attitude towards the situation'. That 'yes' was particularly
memorable: so casual as to be conversational, yet emphatic enough to signal
deliberation.

Exactly a month later, the splendid alliance of Haig and Deng, with Messrs Pol
Pot and Ieng Sary, leaders of the notorious Khmer Rouge which Vietnam ousted
in January 1979, completed a successful rout of world opinion at the United
Nations special conference on Cambodia. Some of the delegates, particularly
those from Southeast Asian countries, were angered at the bullying they received
from the Chinese, and there was something of a crisis until the new French
administration stepped in to mediate. Under Giscard, the French had wisely sat on
their hands. Now Mitterrand regards the restoration of civil life in Cambodia
under Vietnamese auspices as an infamous extension of Soviet influence, and the
UN representative of Eurosocialism shuffled up behind Haig, Deng and Pol Pot,
to help ensure an acceptable resolution. (Apparently Vietnam's joining COME-
CON as China severed aid will now deprive Hanoi of significant French aid, as if
this will lessen the role of the USSR.)

United Nations

Mrs Ieng Thirith (left) speaking at the UN on 13 September 1979. The wife of Ieng Sary and the sister of Pol Pot's wife, she is currently 'The Minister of Social Affairs of Democratic Kampuchea'. Next to her is Mr Thiounn Prasit, the 'Permanent Representative of Democratic Kampuchea' at the UN. He and his brothers, also 'Ministers', are from an elite, historically pro-French family.

There may not be the stomach in the UN for another episode similar to the 20-year exclusion of mainland China in favour of Taiwan. Singapore's plan had been to forge a Cambodian front to replace Pol Pot, at least diplomatically. This would have offered a moderate solution, preserved the fighting, and put the blame on 'obdurate' Hanoi. However, the Chinese presented a violently antagonistic draft resolution, and blocked an invitation to the conference being sent to the Phnom Penh administration of Heng Samrin. It was already known that the Cambodians would not accept a call from any body that included Pol Pot representatives among its number. Nonetheless, Peking argued that the incumbent government was no more than a 'puppet' and could not be regarded as a party to the dispute.

Possibly the Chinese were disturbed by the relative (and peaceful) success of the recent 'elections' in Cambodia. There was no real choice of candidates, of course. The country is typical of Southeast Asia in that respect—as is Singapore. Nonetheless, even the *Financial Times* correspondent, who regards the Vietnamese as 'evil', reported that the 'enthusiasm of many Kampucheans in both town and village for the panoply of electioneering last week was undoubtedly genuine.' Any opening towards a settlement between this Cambodian regime and others in the region is anathema to Peking, which imagines that its own interests will be better served by a protracted war against Vietnam.

At the credentials debate in October 1980, Singapore's representative T. Koh had persuaded the British Ambassador and others that Cambodia was like Afghanistan, and that Vietnam had only complained about the Pol Pot regime after it invaded. In fact, nearly a year before the takeover, Hanoi had offered demilitarisation and international inspection of the Vietnam-Cambodia border. It sent the proposal to the UN which, for all its fine words about peace, could not bestir itself to *prevent* a war. Singapore, at least, was aware of the situation. Its Minister of Defence argued at the time (perhaps not knowing his speech would be published):

> Whether or not the Vietnamese have any intention of forming an Indochinese Federation... the Pol Pot regime's aggressive behaviour and irrational claims to Vietnamese portions of the Mekong delta area gave Hanoi ample reason to initiate military counter-action against the Kampuchean government. The puzzle is this: how did the Chinese come to find themselves committed to supporting Kampuchea in her confrontation with Vietnam?

Today, the puzzle has expanded massively, to include nearly a hundred nations, who send their representatives to cross their hearts and plead their principles before Pol Pot's Foreign Minister Ieng Sary.

The Vietnamese have stated repeatedly that they will withdraw all their troops from Cambodia when China settles with Hanoi and ceases to assail Vietnam. Slowly, other countries seem to be learning that China is indeed the more aggressive party.

Only India has distinguished itself in its policies towards Cambodia and China. It regarded Singapore's efforts to replace Pol Pot while preserving the military assault upon the Vietnamese and Khmer armies as an attempt to get 'milk and meat from the same cow'. It boycotted the conference. It has recognized Heng Samrin. At the same time it has entered talks with China on their own border dispute, and will begin cultural exchanges. Mrs Gandhi has in principle agreed to visit Peking. By chance, the policy which best suits India's own interests is also the most principled approach: the way to normality in Cambodia lies in overcoming China's siege mentality, rather than feeding it US-style, while making absolutely no concessions towards Pol Pot.

(31 July 1981)

THE 1981 VOTE

Spain, Jamaica and the United Arab Emirates were among seven countries that switched their votes to Pol Pot at the UN in 1981. When the United Nations General Assembly voted on 18 September to continue its endorsement of the Khmer Rouge regime, those in favour of Pol Pot increased from 74 to 77. Jamaica was alone in switching its vote from favouring removal of Pol Pot to favouring endorsement. Along with Spain and the United Arab Emirates, Botswana, Central African Republic, the Ivory Coast and Swaziland came off the fence to vote for endorsement. Chad, Sierra Leone and the Solomon Islands shifted from abstention to favouring removal of Pol Pot. Among those who last year supported his endorsement, Australia, Barbados, the Bahamas and Cameroons switched to abstention this time.

The vote was taken swiftly, after the beginning of the new UN session. The day before the delegations assembled, the United States announced that it had evidence—which it could not confirm—that a poisonous yellow powder had been found on a leaf in... Cambodia. There were lots of big headlines and Mrs Kirkpatrick, Reagan's UN representative, successfully demanded an international enquiry.

(2 October 1981)

Part VI
From Vietnam
to El Salvador

Heroes
John Pilger

'Fats' was shot in 1967, and I feel ashamed that I have long since forgotten his name. He lay with his stunned, bleached face and his sergeant, trying to stem a crescendo of screams, which were heard through the night and dawn and remain as memorable as the place where he fell: a trench in which were stacked boxes of toothbrushes, thousands of them, and party balloons and portable electric flush lavatories, all puce coloured, and New York cut steaks packed in dry ice. Fats was a United States Marine, a 'grunt' in a Combined Action Company, better known as a 'hearts and minds' unit. The toothbrushes, balloons and lavatories were to win the hearts and minds of Vietnamese villagers in 'Indian country': the steak was for the next day's barbecue in honour of a colonel who had promised to bring out beer for 'my boys who never say die'. In the colonel's office in Danang were the framed words: 'Grab 'em by the balls and their hearts and minds will follow'. Lyndon Johnson is alleged to have coined that.

One year later I looked up Fats's sergeant in upstate New York and found him on a porch, coming out of a bender. He had uttered barely a word about the war since his return home with a piece of shrapnel, knife-shaped, in his neck because nobody wanted to listen. To former friends in the peace movement he was a pariah or a dupe or a child-killer; to his own community he was obsolete; to his family he was an embarrassment, though they never said as much.

He came home just as the Vietcong were storming the American embassy in Saigon and Walter Cronkite was handing down a televised tablet to the nation: 'Thou shalt no longer support this war, for it is lost'. Fats, he reported, was 'in some bad VA hospital, dead up to his neck'. Both men had volunteered for the Marines, having been weaned on John Wayne, to whom Jimmy Carter felt moved to give some ridiculous posthumous medal and who never saw action in any war. Both men were decorated and given a disability allowance that would keep them in Kentucky fried chicken and little else. Both men had fussed protectively over me, a terrified civilian in their midst, when half the village turned into Vietcong and had come over the wire, bearing hearts and minds and AK-47s.

When they left for Vietnam they were American winners—the kind John Wayne evangelists were proud of; now they were losers and among the first to be drafted into a great invisible army assigned to a purgatory of silence, shame, indifference. In 1979 a national poll found that 62 per cent of American people believed that veterans of Vietnam 'fought in the wrong war, in the wrong place, at the wrong time, and were suckers'.

Vietnam was the longest war this century, in which more Marines died than during all of World War Two, and 80 per cent of all those who served were volunteers. There is not a single national monument to the dead of that war, nor has there been a great parade of the kind America relishes; of the kind given to the 52 American 'heroes' held hostage in Iran and then celebrated relentlessly, although their faces were unzapped by the 'friendly fire' of Napalm and their testicles were intact and their body cells undisturbed by cancers resulting from chemical warfare. When a group of disabled Vietnam veterans took their hurt to the White House, President Carter was 'unavailable'. One of his media men, in a loud aside, said, 'You have got to understand these guys are a no-votes situation'. Bob Muller, in his wheelchair, heard that.

I never met Bob Muller in Vietnam, but I vividly remember him being thrown out of the Republican Party's nomination circus for Richard Nixon in 1972—in his wheelchair. Bob Muller, a Marine lieutenant, having lost the use of his legs and gained a chest-load of ribbons and medals, was a Grade-A hero: but, alas, there he was spoiling it all by bellowing at Nixon that the war was unwinnable and genocidal. Seven years later I saw this hero again, shrunken and more fragile now, on the steps of New York's City Hall.

It was a Memorial Day and there were uniforms and salutes and dignitaries, although Bob Muller's was the only broken body in view. He had hold of a microphone and within seconds had silenced even the construction site beyond the crowd. 'Listen to me!' he commanded, 'there are 280,000 veterans of Vietnam in New York alone, and a *third* of them can't find jobs. Throughout America *sixty per cent* of all black combat veterans are unemployed. Almost *half* of all combat veterans are either alcoholics or addicted to drugs, or in pain in the head and just as many are probably dying now from the poisons we dumped over there as died in the battlefield. You people out there ran a number on us, right? Your guilt, your hangups make you walk away from us; we wear artificial legs so *you* won't know we're disabled veterans. Why do we feel like we just held up a bank when someone asks us about our wounds? Why do we feel that, if we believe in America, we must be guilty for letting America down or, if we're critical of America, we can't explain even to ourselves why we went over there and needlessly killed civilians? Eight of my friends, with legs like these, killed themselves when they got home; we've got the *highest* suicide rate in America... and that's all I want to say to you today'.

Bob Muller now runs Vietnam Veterans of America from an almost bare office adjacent to a wholesaler of dolls, at the seedy end of Fifth Avenue. There is seldom enough money to pay the telephone bill, in contrast with the Government Veterans Administration, which devotes much of its powerfully-lobbied budget to the running of a chain of nursing homes, mostly for veterans of the two world wars and Korea: the 'winners'. The statistics Bob Muller punched at the Memorial Day assembly included those borne out by a five-volume study by the Centre for Policy Research in New York and commissioned by the Veterans Association. The results made such a mockery of previous official estimates of the distress of Vietnam veterans that the government 'lost' the report until Muller's organisation forced its release under the Freedom of Information Act. The study found that more than a third of Vietnam veterans were suffering from 'delayed stress syndrome'—a slow-fuse psychological disturbance quite distinct from the 'shell shock' and 'combat fatigue' of the world wars, and unique to the Vietnam experience of terror, atrocities and guilt sustained in the cause of nothing.

Alonza Gibbs, whom I met in Philadelphia, was blown up by mortar fire and suffered multiple gunshot wounds. He said that a third of his company had been wiped out by inept air strikes ordered by the company commander. (This was not uncommon: thus the term 'friendly fire'.) He watched Vietnamese prisoners interrogated, then thrown out of helicopters and others laced together with a detonating cord which, when pulled, blew their heads off. 'We had a battalion commander who is a general now', he said. 'I believe he's a cissy. He issued all of us with hatchets and offered a case of whisky to the first man to chop somebody's head off. And, sure enough, a head got chopped off. Some of his boys are right here now, crazier than bed bugs'.

Decorated for trying to save the life of a comrade, Alonza Gibbs now seldom sleeps, is in constant pain from his wounds, drinks too much and suffers, almost certainly, from delayed stress syndrome. 'His personality is completely changed', says his sister, with whom he lives. He fought in Vietnam in 1965 and says that a Veterans Administration doctor told him, 'There is nothing wrong with you that a young man won't snap out of'. In the last two years he has received about £20 a month. 'I didn't like to face up to it at first,' he said, 'but the fact is if I go for a job and tell the man I was in Vietnam, I don't get the job'.

This rejection by employers is also part of the 'Vietnam syndrome'. After World War Two it was deemed a 'patriotic duty' to employ a returned soldier. By comparison, most of the Vietnam veterans I interviewed spoke of not getting a job, regardless of their qualifications, whenever they listed their service record— 'in the time honoured way', as one veteran put it, 'that blacks are politely turned down'. One veteran was told outright: 'This plant is not taking on any Vietnam dope addicts'. Mike Sulsona, a New York double amputee, wears artificial legs, with pain, chiefly because he wishes to disguise the fact he is a disabled Vietnam veteran. 'When I'm in the wheelchair', he said, 'I'm asked about my legs and if I say "Vietnam" the embarrassment and at times hostility is too much to take.'

World War Two and Korea veterans were 'rewarded' with the GI Bill which Lyndon Johnson reluctantly re-introduced in 1966, but with a catch: it gave Vietnam veterans £1500 a year *less* than their fathers received more than 30 years earlier. In 1972 Nixon vetoed the Veterans Medical Care Expansion Act, calling it 'fiscally irresponsible and inflationary'. The United States then had spent some $165 billion pursuing its task of human and environmental vandalism in Southeast Asia, which Ronald Reagan was to call, in 1980, 'our noble cause'.

'I was an infantry officer', said Bob Muller, 'I had the battleship New Jersey fire in support of me in the DMZ. I had jet strikes one after the other. I had an hour and a half of heavy artillery many, many times. It was *routine* for me to spend £100,000 a day to kill people. Then I get shot in the process, come back home and my government tells me it's fiscally irresponsible and inflationary to provide adequate medical care in the hospital! Can you imagine what that does to us?'

What that does to them is to punish them for losing and, worse, for *admitting* failure and for shouting the secret of Vietnam: that it was a war of rampant, experimental technology against a peasant people who were, from the beginning, racially expendable. Not a 'mistake' as the tribunes of the American liberal consensus, now gone to ground, used to say; but a crime without the finale of a Nuremberg. The veterans 'punishment' continued under Jimmy Carter who, in his first fireside chat as President, promised 'top priority' to creating jobs for disabled veterans. Out of 21,000 seriously disabled veterans, 500 were offered work. During last year's Presidential election campaigns, Ronald Reagan said: 'To me it's the height of hypocrisy for the Carter administration to repeatedly tell us how much we owe our Vietnam veterans, then recommend a stingy ten per cent increase in the GI Bill. They deserve pure gratitude, our respect and our continuing concern...'

Last March, President Reagan asked Congress to cut the few programmes designed to help Vietnam veterans find jobs, finish their education and be treated for drug addiction and alcoholism. Ninety-one 'Outreach' programme counselling centres, many of them in the poorest parts of cities and towns, have become a small salvation to many veterans. David Stockman, who runs Reagan's Office of Management and Budget, who evaded the draft by confining himself to divinity school, wants to close them all down.

Reagan's elevation of the Vietnam war as a 'noble cause' which 'ought to have been won' and the relegation of those who bear the war's truth to the boweries of the nation fits nicely into the 'gameplan' for the next 'noble cause'. And if that one fails it, too, can be absolved as a 'tragic mistake.' Vengeance for the humiliation in Vietnam has dominated American global strategy since the day, six years ago, when Ambassador Graham Martin and his poodle were lifted by helicopter out of the US embassy in Saigon. Since then, three administrations have worked to restore the United States from Nixon's memorable 'pitiless giant' to Reagan's 'shining house on the hill'. Reading the newspapers now, deleting Vietnam and writing in El Salvador, the stories seem uncannily similar. In a front page report in the *New York Times* of 28 July 1964, headlined 'US To Enlarge Vietnam Force by 5000 Advisers', there is this gem: 'There was still no sign of a United States decision to carry the war into North Vietnam or throw American units into combat'. In the *Daily Telegraph* of 5 March 1981, under the headline 'No Combat Troops for Salvador,' there is the news that Congress will not block the sending of additional military advisers to El Salvador and that President Reagan sees 'no likelihood' of US troops going into combat.

Like Kennedy, Johnson, Nixon and Ford then, Haig and Reagan now see the world in the same obsessional and obtuse terms, speaking of dominoes as if nations were mere blocks of wood, not complex societies riven with profound differences and cultural animosities. 'It isn't just El Salvador', said Reagan. 'That happens to be the target at the moment. Our problem is in this whole hemisphere and keeping this sort of thing out'. Johnson and Nixon spoke almost precisely those words; only the geography changed.

Perhaps the lies that power the escalator going up to the inevitable are more obvious now, but the escalator keeps moving. Indeed, the fabled 'line' that was drawn in Vietnam 'to stop the advance of Chinese communism' is being drawn once again, this time to keep out the forces of 'Soviet-backed international terrorism' in Central America which mysteriously threaten the most powerful nation on earth.

No matter that armed and battle-ready exiled foreign 'freedom fighters'—surely international terrorists by the White House's standards—are training openly, and illegally, in Florida. No matter that even the CIA, in common with other US intelligence groups, has questioned the catch-all charge against Moscow that it is running the international terrorist show, because the Soviet Union is as much beset by 'terrorism' as any other adventurous imperial power: for example, in Afghanistan and Eritrea where it is using weapons and tactics studiously copied

Camera Press

Syndication International

Weaned on John Wayne: new recruits, training completed, prepare to set off for Vietnam (above); the aftermath (below): veterans demonstrate on Capitol steps, 27 April 1971.

from the Americans in Vietnam—yet another brutal irony. No matter that the former American ambassador in El Salvador, Robert White, has told a Congressional hearing that the war in that country is caused by social injustice and that the real terrorists are the regime backed by Haig and Reagan. 'The security forces in El Salvador have been responsible for the deaths of thousands and thousands of young people', said White, 'and they have executed them on the mere suspicion that they are leftists or sympathise with leftists. Are we *really* going to be part of all that...?' No matter that the Reagan administration's real aim is to be seen 'hanging tough', as Nixon used to say, in a little country where the options are soft and the fodder is plentiful.

The policy of hanging tough, partly to justify a war economy and partly in the cause of vengeance, is double-handed: while adventure is pursued in El Salvador (and, less obtrusively, in much of Central America) revenge is exacted in Vietnam itself. The Reagan administration's commitment to 'another Vietnam' is deeper than those Americans who oppose it realise; and it is not purely American. According to the excellent Center for International Policy in Washington, $523 million will go to the El Salvador junta after Washington applies its persuasive powers to the World Bank, the Inter-American Development Bank and the International Monetary Fund and after it 'harnesses' the European donors, regardless of their public utterances of distaste for the new adventure. Not that the Thatcher government has uttered any such distaste. Indeed, which government is likely to give more money than any European government, more than Canada, more than Argentina and Brazil, to a regime patently guilty of murdering its own people? Margaret Thatcher's government, of course.

Half a world away, in Vietnam, about which we hear little these days, there is the beginning of famine. Six million Vietnamese are faced with 'serious malnutrition', according to a UN Food and Agricultural Organisation group. Rations are now less than ever during the war years: less than half the daily amount of food needed for a healthy survival. General Haig has now said publicly that the United States intends to 'squeeze' Vietnam in every way: 'de-stabilisation' once more. The Japanese and the EEC have sent no relief: Britain long ago cut off its piddling humanitarian aid.

In May 1981 China carried out a 'punitive' action against Vietnam's northern border, similar to its attack in 1979 which had prior American approval. Last week the 'landbridge' from Thailand to Cambodia was re-opened, allowing Western, chiefly American sustenance to flow more conveniently to Pol Pot's Khmer Rouge and thus to accelerate the 'de-stabilisation' of Cambodia and Vietnam and to push both countries deeper into the arms of the Soviet Union, which neither wants. In Cu Chi, near Saigon, which I remember as thick forest, there is today a shimmering horizon of wilderness which has been poisoned, perhaps for generations. Eleven million gallons of the herbicide Agent Orange were dumped on Vietnam; its chief ingredient, dioxin, is estimated to be a thousand times more destructive than thalidomide. Blind and deformed babies are now common in those areas sprayed during Operation Hades, later re-named Operation Ranch Hand.

Charlie Hartz, a Vietnam veteran who was exposed to Agent Orange, is going blind and is dying from cancer. His four children were born deformed. He is one of many veterans similarly afflicted, and none of them has been compensated. In Beallsville, Ohio, Betty Rucker still has the telegram which told her that her son, Rick, was killed by 'a friendly rocket'. When Rick went off to war, Mrs Rucker

thought Vietnam was 'somewhere near Cuba or Panama, real close and threatening'. Considering events today, her remark, made to me a decade ago, is searing in
its irony.

Indeed, as we now know, US 'advisers' have arrived in that very region, and
more are to follow, but of course they will only shoot their guns in self-defence,
just as it was in Vietnam, in the beginning. And if they do find themselves shooting
their guns, they will need to be 'protected'; and then there is the 'likelihood' if not
the certainty that a new generation of heroes, the Ricks and Bobs, the Charlies
and Fats, will be on their way.

(22 May 1981)